ROCKETRY

Investigate the Science and Technology of Rockets and Ballistics

Carla Mooney

Illustrated by Caitlin Denham

~ Latest titles in the *Build It Yourself* Series ~

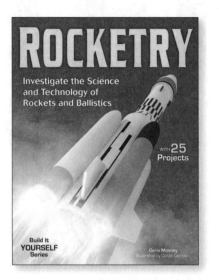

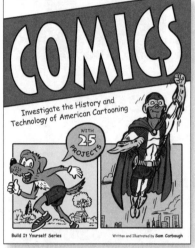

Check out more titles at www.nomadpress.net

Nomad Press
A division of Nomad Communications
10 9 8 7 6 5 4 3 2 1

This book was manufactured by TC Transcontinental Printing,
Beauceville Québec, Canada
August 2014, Job #67281

ISBN Softcover: 978-1-61930-236-5
ISBN Hardcover: 978-1-61930-232-7

Illustrations by Caitlin Denham
Educational Consultant, Marla Conn

Questions regarding the ordering of this book should be addressed to
Nomad Press
2456 Christian St.
White River Junction, VT 05001
www.nomadpress.net

Printed in Canada.

CONTENTS

INTERESTED IN PRIMARY SOURCES?

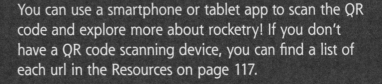

Look for this icon.

PS

You can use a smartphone or tablet app to scan the QR code and explore more about rocketry! If you don't have a QR code scanning device, you can find a list of each url in the Resources on page 117.

TIMELINE

AROUND 400 BCE
The ancient Greeks invent a flying wooden pigeon using the principle of action and reaction, which is the basis of all rocket engines.

AROUND 60 CE
Greek engineer and mathematician Hero of Alexandria creates an aeolipile, a spinning ball that uses the same principle of action and reaction.

AROUND 600
The Chinese create fire arrows, the first gunpowder-based rockets, for use in fireworks celebrations.

1865
French author Jules Verne publishes *From the Earth to the Moon*, which interests many in space travel.

1846
English inventor William Hale improves rocket accuracy with vanes.

1903
Russian Konstantin Tsiolkovsky publishes a paper, *Investigation of World Spaces by Reactive Vehicles*, which lays the groundwork for modern rocketry.

1907
American Robert Goddard builds his first experimental rocket.

1923
Hermann Oberth publishes *The Rocket into Planetary Space*.

1926
Goddard successfully fires the world's first liquid-propellant rocket.

1927
The Society for Space Travel is founded in Germany.

TIMELINE

1232
The Chinese use fire arrow rockets in a battle against the Mongols.

1379
Rockets are documented for the first time in Europe at the siege of Chioggia, Italy.

1429
The French army uses gunpowder rockets to defend the city of Orleans.

1804
Sir William Congreve begins development of British military rockets.

1687
Physicist and mathematician Sir Isaac Newton publishes his work, *Philosophiae Naturalis Principia Mathematica*, which provides the foundation for understanding a rocket's motion.

1814
American Francis Scott Key writes of "the rocket's red glare" as the British fire Congreve's rockets on Fort McHenry in Baltimore Harbor during the War of 1812.

1931
Johannes Winkler launches Europe's first successful liquid-fuel rocket.

The German army forms a department of rocket research to develop war weapons.

1942
German engineers successfully launch the A-4 rocket—later renamed the V-2.

1945
After Germany surrenders, German rocket scientists move to the United States and the Soviet Union to continue rocket research.

1944
The Germans mass produce the V-2 rocket and launch it against England and Belgium in World War II.

TIMELINE

1949

Americans launch the first Viking rocket based on the V-2 design.

1957

The Soviets launch *Sputnik*, the first artificial satellite sent into space, marking the beginning of the space race between the Soviet Union and the United States.

Sputnik 2 carries Laika the dog, the first living creature into space.

1958

The United States sends *Explorer 1*, the first U.S. satellite, into space and establishes the National Aeronautics and Space Administration (NASA) to operate its space program.

1973

NASA sends the Skylab space station into space.

1972

NASA's *Apollo 17* is the last mission to the moon in the twentieth century.

1971

The Soviets create the world's first space station.

1977

The first space shuttle, *Enterprise*, makes a successful suborbital flight.

1986

Six astronauts and teacher Christa McAuliffe die in the space shuttle *Challenger* disaster.

1995

Work begins on the International Space Station.

1981

The first manned space shuttle, *Columbia*, is launched into space.

1983

Sally Ride becomes the first American woman in space.

TIMELINE

1961

Russian cosmonaut Yuri Gagarin becomes the first human in space on April 12. American astronaut Alan Shepard is the first American in space on May 5.

1962

Astronaut John Glenn becomes the first American to orbit the earth in the capsule *Friendship 7*.

1966

The Soviets achieve the first soft lunar landing on the moon with *Luna 9*.

1967

Three American astronauts die in an accidental fire inside the *Apollo 1* spacecraft during a training exercise.

1969

American astronauts Neil Armstrong and Buzz Aldrin fly on *Apollo 11* and become the first humans to step onto the Moon.

1970

The *Apollo 13* mission is forced to abort its trip to the moon and return to Earth.

2004

The *Cassini* spacecraft arrives at Saturn to begin a four-year mission of scientific research.

2000

The Advanced Space Propulsion Lab introduces the VASIMR, a high-speed rocket that may be able to take astronauts to Mars.

2003

The space shuttle *Columbia* disintegrates on re-entry and all seven crew members die.

2001

NASA launches the *Mars Odyssey* mission. The spacecraft successfully orbits Mars.

1981–2010

NASA space shuttles use reusable solid rocket boosters.

— INTRODUCTION —
BLAST OFF!

Have you ever seen the **launch** of a **rocket**? While the imposing rocket rests on the **launch pad**, it looms larger than a 10-story building. Then the countdown begins. "T minus 15 seconds and counting . . . ten, nine . . . ignition sequence start . . . six, five, four . . ."

WORDS TO KNOW

launch: to fire up into the air.

rocket: a machine that pushes itself forward by pushing out material such as hot gas.

launch pad: the platform from which a rocket launches.

speed of sound: the speed at which sound travels. In the air at sea level, this is 755 miles per hour (1,215 kilometers per hour).

The rocket's engines come to life with a roar. Steam pours from the rocket's base. The rocket rises slowly, lifting its massive body straight into the air. With flames shooting from its tail, the rocket blasts into the sky. In less than a minute, it is traveling faster than the **speed of sound**.

As the rocket's solid-**fuel boosters** burn out, they detach from the main rocket body and fall away. A few minutes later, the rocket's first **stage** detaches and is discarded. The second stage ignites. About 10 minutes after launch, the rocket and its **payload** are in space.

> **ROCKETRY IS THE DESIGN, CONSTRUCTION, OPERATION, AND LAUNCHING OF ROCKETS.**

Welcome to the amazing world of rocketry! Not long ago, rockets could only be found in science fiction. Today, real rockets are the fastest, most powerful **vehicles** on Earth and in outer space.

WHAT IS A ROCKET?

A rocket is a machine that pushes itself forward by **expelling** material such as hot gas. Rockets come in many sizes and are used in different ways.

The first known rockets were military rockets carrying explosive **warheads** to attack enemy positions and **infrastructure**. The smallest military rocket can be launched from a handheld launcher. Massive **missiles** can be launched from one continent and hit a target on another continent.

WORDS TO KNOW

fuel: a material used to produce heat or power.

booster: a rocket used to give another craft the power needed for takeoff.

stage: a smaller rocket that is stacked with other rockets and detaches when its fuel is used up.

payload: the **cargo** of a rocket, such as an explosive charge, instruments, or **astronauts**.

cargo: goods or materials that are carried or transported by a vehicle.

astronaut: a person trained for spaceflight.

vehicle: a machine that moves people and things from one place to another.

expel: to drive or push out.

warhead: the part of a missile that holds an explosive charge.

infrastructure: basic facilities such as roads, power plants, and communication systems.

missile: an object or weapon that is **propelled** toward a target.

propel: to drive or move forward.

Military rockets can be launched from the ground or from a vehicle. Ships, submarines, helicopters, fighter jets, and land vehicles can launch military rockets.

Some rockets are launch vehicles. A launch vehicle carries a payload, such as people, **satellites**, or **robot probes** into space. Satellite launch vehicles put satellites into **orbit** around the earth. These satellites are used for many things, including weather forecasting, entertainment, research, and communications. Some rocket launch vehicles carry scientific equipment and probes into space to study planets, galaxies, stars, and other **astronomical** objects.

WORDS TO KNOW

satellite: an object that orbits another object in space.

robot probe: a machine that travels into space to find out more about space and send information back to the earth.

orbit: the path of an object circling another object in space.

astronomical: having to do with things in outer space.

mass: the amount of **matter** in an object.

matter: anything that has weight and takes up space.

gravity: the force that holds objects on the ground.

SOME OF THE MOST EXCITING ROCKET LAUNCHES ARE THE ONES THAT CARRY ASTRONAUTS INTO SPACE.

Rockets that transport astronauts and their equipment need to lift the most weight. Weight is the product of the **mass** of an object and the force of **gravity** acting on the object. It takes a lot of fuel to lift a heavy load and carry it for a long distance. A bigger rocket is needed to carry all that fuel.

DID YOU KNOW?

In 1970, a rocket engine powered a car called the Blue Flame. The car shot to a speed of 622 miles per hour (1,001 kilometers per hour).

Experts in many different areas are needed to create rockets, including science, **technology**, **engineering**, and math. Scientists who study **physics**, chemistry, **aeronautics**, mechanical engineering, and mathematics all contribute to our understanding of rocketry.

WORDS TO KNOW

technology: tools, methods, and systems used to solve a problem or do work.

engineering: using science and math to design and build things.

physics: the science of matter, motion, force, and **energy**.

energy: the ability to do work.

aeronautics: the science of flight.

orbiter: a spacecraft designed to orbit a planet or moon without landing on its surface.

ROCKETRY IS ALSO A POPULAR HOBBY.

Kids and adults enjoy making their own rockets from kits or from parts they build themselves. Many interesting rocket designs have been built by amateur rocket builders in their own homes or with other people in rocketry clubs.

THE SPACE SHUTTLE

The space shuttle is a rocket that was built to be used several times. The shuttle has an **orbiter**, an external tank, and two solid rocket boosters. It flies into space like other rockets but, unlike other rockets, the space shuttle's orbiter has wings like an airplane. The wings allow it to land without engine power. The space shuttle's solid rocket boosters are also reusable. After they are used, the rocket boosters fall into the ocean and are recovered so they can be used again on future missions. Each booster can be used several times.

PS You can watch the spaceship shuttle *Discovery* take off and drop its solid rocket boosters.

MAKE YOUR OWN ROCKETS

The activities in *Rocketry: Investigate the Science and Technology of Rockets and Ballistics* will help you understand the science behind rockets. Like rocket scientists, you'll apply concepts of physics, chemistry, **aerodynamics**, and mathematics to design your own rockets. You'll test how different designs affect performance and discover how rockets get their power. After exploring the technology that sends astronauts and spacecraft into space, you'll even learn about rockets of the future that scientists are working on today.

Most of the activities in this book require no special equipment or tools. You can use ordinary household materials and parts. That way you can build a simple, do-it-yourself rocket model without spending a lot of money. Have fun!

WORDS TO KNOW

aerodynamics: the movement of air and other gases around an object.

ROCKETRY SAFETY TIPS

- **Ask permission before launching any rockets.** You may need an adult to help you with certain sections of this book's activities.

- **Wear eye protection.** Safety goggles can be found at any hardware store.

- **Launch the rocket outside.** Model rockets can travel considerable distances at high rates of speed. Set up your launch pad outside, where you have plenty of room for the rocket to fly. Make sure it is not pointed toward any people, animals, buildings, or other structures.

— CHAPTER 1 —
THE DEVELOPMENT OF ROCKETRY

It might surprise you to learn that rockets have been blasting off for centuries. The first rockets were very simple, much like today's fireworks. But over time rockets have become so complex that we use them to launch weapons and travel into outer space. Scientists have discovered new fuels to power rockets, better ways to control rocket flight, and new ways to use rockets. Can you think of some ways rockets have been a part of your life?

ANCIENT GREECE

Ancient Greeks created some of the first rocket-like devices powered by steam. Around 400 **BCE**, a Greek named Archytas created a wooden bird that flew along a wire, pushed by steam.

WORDS TO KNOW

BCE: put after a date, BCE stands for Before Common Era and counts down to zero. CE stands for Common Era and counts up from zero. These non-religious terms correspond to BC and AD.

Almost 500 years later, another Greek, named Hero, created a steam-powered rocket he called an **aeolipile**. First, Hero boiled water in a kettle to create steam. The steam traveled up two pipes to a **sphere**, which had L-shaped tubes on opposite sides to release the steam. As the steam escaped the L-shaped tubes, it provided a **force** that pushed against the sphere and caused it to **rotate**.

Hero's aeolipile worked because of Isaac Newton's third law of **motion**, that every action has an opposite and equal reaction. We'll talk more about Newton's laws of motion in Chapter 2.

CHINESE FIRE ARROWS

Many people believe that the first true rockets were developed by the Chinese, who discovered how to make a simple gunpowder. They mixed **saltpeter** with sulfur and carbon. This mixture was nicknamed *huo yao* (pronounced "hwaw yow"), which meant flaming medicine. The Chinese filled hollow **bamboo** tubes with the gunpowder mixture. When tossed into a fire, these tubes exploded impressively.

WORDS TO KNOW

aeolipile: a spinning ball invented by Greek mathematician Hero that uses steam to move.

sphere: round, like a ball.

force: a push or pull that changes the speed or direction of an object.

rotate: to turn like a wheel around a fixed point.

motion: the act or process of moving.

saltpeter: a white powder found in Chinese caves that was used in early Chinese gunpowder.

bamboo: a tree-like type of grass with a hollow, woody stem.

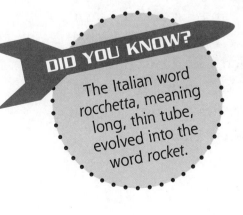

DID YOU KNOW?

The Italian word rocchetta, meaning long, thin tube, evolved into the word rocket.

The Chinese used these first fireworks at religious ceremonies and celebration festivals. They experimented with the design of their exploding fireworks by attaching the bamboo tubes to arrows.

IF THEY SEALED ONE END OF THE TUBE AND LIT THE GUNPOWDER, THE FIRE, SMOKE, AND GAS THAT ESCAPED THE TUBE'S OPEN END SHOT THE ARROW FORWARD.

WORDS TO KNOW

Mongols: a group of wandering tribes led by Genghis Khan that lived to the north of China.

nomadic: moving from place to place each season in search of food and water.

tribe: a large group of people with common ancestors and customs.

Although the fire arrows were not very accurate, they made a loud explosion. This proved to be very good at frightening enemy armies, such as the **Mongols**. The Mongols were a group of **nomadic tribes** that lived to the north of China. Several tribes joined to form the Mongol Empire, led by a fierce warrior named Genghis Khan.

In 1232, the Mongols attacked the Chinese. To repel the invaders, the Chinese launched their fire arrow rockets during the battle of Kai-Keng. At first, the fire arrows frightened the Mongol warriors and spooked their horses. But the Mongol soldiers learned how to make their own fire arrows to use against their enemies.

ROCKETS MOVE WEST

The Mongols brought fire arrows west with them through Asia and Europe. During the 1200s, several Europeans experimented with rockets and rocket science, creating both weapons and fireworks for entertainment. An English monk named Roger Bacon worked to improve the gunpowder that powered rockets and increase the rocket's **range**. In France, writer Jean Froissart correctly suggested that rockets would travel in a straighter path if fired out of a tube.

By the 1500s, rockets were still used in Europe, mostly as fireworks. Then a fireworks maker in Germany named Johann Schmidlap invented a step rocket that could fly higher than earlier rockets.

WORDS TO KNOW

range: the distance a rocket can travel.

artillery: large guns used to shoot over a great distance.

multi-stage rocket: a rocket that is made up of smaller rockets that detach as their fuel is used up.

STAGE 3

STAGE 2

STAGE 1

Schmidlap's rocket was powered by multiple explosions, or stages. The first stage lifted the rocket off the ground. A second stage exploded and propelled the rocket even higher in the air. Schmidlap's **multi-stage rocket** design would become the basic design for modern rockets that fly into outer space.

DID YOU KNOW?

British **artillery** expert Colonel William Congreve designed rockets for the British military during the late 1700s and early 1800s. During the War of 1812, British warships fired rockets on America's Fort McHenry. Watching the battle inspired Francis Scott Key to write the line "the rocket's red glare" in "The Star-Spangled Banner."

Sir Isaac Newton was a scientist who lived during the 1600s. He introduced three laws of motion that form the **foundation** of modern rocket science and explain how and why rockets work. **Newton's three basic laws are as follows.**

1. An object will remain at rest or at a constant **velocity** unless an external force acts upon it.

2. An object's velocity will change when an external force acts upon it.

3. Every action has an equal and opposite reaction.

WORDS TO KNOW

foundation: the basis of something.

velocity: the rate at which an object is moving.

NEWTON'S WORK HELPED SCIENTISTS UNDERSTAND HOW ROCKETS LAUNCH AND FLY IN SPACE.

His laws inspired scientists to experiment with new rocket designs. They used their new understanding of motion to create designs that improved rocket performance and control.

Although rockets had been used as weapons across Europe, they were not very accurate. Rockets often exploded too soon. An army could fire thousands of rockets at the enemy, but not be sure of where they would land. More reliable artillery were the battlefield weapons of choice. But rockets returned to the battlefield in the twentieth century, when better control systems made them more useful.

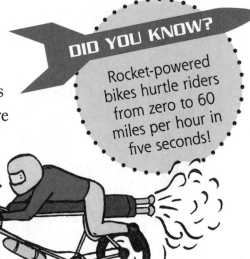

DID YOU KNOW?

Rocket-powered bikes hurtle riders from zero to 60 miles per hour in five seconds!

FATHERS OF MODERN ROCKETRY

In 1898, a Russian schoolteacher named Konstantin Tsiolkovsky suggested that rockets could be used to explore outer space. He believed that a rocket's speed and height were only limited by the **exhaust velocity** of the escaping gases. The exhaust velocity is a result of the explosive force of the rocket fuel. The more powerful the fuel's explosion, the greater the **thrust**.

At the time, rockets used solid **propellants** to generate enough force to launch. Tsiolkovsky believed that a liquid propellant would provide a greater force and allow the rocket to fly higher, perhaps high enough to reach outer space. He wrote scientific articles that encouraged readers to think about designing rockets that could carry humans into space. Because of his ideas about rockets and rocket science, Tsiolkovsky is known as the "Father of Modern Astronautics." Yet because much of his work was written in Russian, rocket scientists outside of Russia did not know of it for many years.

In the early twentieth century, American Robert H. Goddard was also experimenting with rockets. At the time, most people believed that rockets needed to push against air in order to fly, but Goddard believed that rockets could fly in a **vacuum**. Why is this important? You'll find out in the next chapter!

WORDS TO KNOW

exhaust velocity: the speed at which gas escapes from a rocket.

thrust: the force created when gas escapes from a rocket's engine.

propellant: a combination of fuel and **oxidizer** that burns to produce thrust in a rocket.

oxidizer: a substance that contains oxygen that mixes with fuel in a rocket engine to help it burn.

vacuum: a space in which there is no air.

GODDARD SET UP AN EXPERIMENT TO TEST ROCKET FLIGHT IN A VACUUM.

Air Resistance

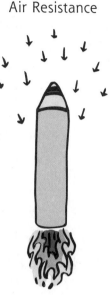

He built a chamber, removed the air from it, and put a small rocket inside the chamber. Goddard fired the rocket successfully, proving that rockets could fly in a vacuum.

Goddard also noted that the rocket **accelerated** faster in the vacuum than it did when launched in the air. He believed this happened because there was no **resistance** in the vacuum. There was no **air resistance** to push against the rocket and slow its acceleration.

No Air Resistance (vacuum)

At first, Goddard worked with solid fuels. He tested several types and measured the exhaust velocity of each. Eventually, Goddard came to the same conclusion as Tsiolkovsky, that solid fuels could not provide enough power to launch rockets into space. He too believed that liquid fuel could create a more powerful thrust.

WORDS TO KNOW

accelerate: to change the speed of an object over time.

resistance: a force that slows down another force.

air resistance: the frictional force that acts on an object as it travels through the air.

rocketeer: a person who designs, launches, operates, or travels in a space rocket.

TEENAGE ROCKETEER

In 1908, at age 14, German **rocketeer** Hermann Oberth designed his first model rocket. In 1923, Oberth wrote a paper called *The Rocket into Planetary Space*. In 1929, he expanded the paper to include the idea that one day rockets would be so powerful they could carry a man into space. His book inspired the formation of many small rocket societies around the world.

At the time, no one had built a successful rocket that used liquid fuel. This was partly because rockets that use liquid fuel are much more complex than rockets that use solid fuel. They need many parts, including fuel and oxygen tanks, pumps, and **combustion chambers**.

After more experiments and testing, on March 16, 1926, Goddard launched the first successful flight of a rocket that used liquid fuel. Goddard's rocket was powered by liquid oxygen and gasoline. It flew for 2½ seconds, reached an **altitude** of 41 feet (12½ meters), and landed 184 feet (56 meters) away.

Goddard's liquid rocket launched a new age of rocketry. He continued his experiments for many years, using bigger rockets that flew higher. He also developed several improvements to rocketry, including a **gyroscope** system for flight control. He added a compartment to a rocket that could hold scientific instruments. He also designed a parachute **recovery system** that allowed a rocket and the scientific instruments it carried to return to Earth safely after flight.

WORDS TO KNOW

combustion: the process of burning.

combustion chamber: the part of a rocket where liquid fuel and oxidizer are combined to create a **chemical reaction**.

chemical reaction: the change of a substance into a new substance.

altitude: the height of something in relation to sea level.

gyroscope: a spinning wheel that is used to help control a rocket in flight.

recovery system: the parts of a rocket that help it return safely to Earth.

Although they never met, Tsiolkovsky, Goddard, and Oberth have been called the fathers of modern rocketry. Despite the fact that at first they knew nothing about each other's research, they still came to many of the same conclusions independently. All three believed that liquid fuel was the key to sending rockets into space.

DID YOU KNOW?

Ballistics is the science that studies the movement of objects that are shot through the air, such as bullets and rockets.

GERMAN ADVANCEMENT

Inspired by Hermann Oberth's 1923 paper, many small rocket societies formed in countries around the world, including Germany, the Soviet Union, and the United States. In Germany, one society was called the Verein fur Raumschiffahrt (VfR) or the Society for Space Travel. Oberth was one of the group's earliest members. Under his guidance, the VfR successfully tested a liquid-fuel rocket. By 1932, VfR members were regularly launching rockets. Another young German, Wernher von Braun, joined the VfR and assisted Oberth with rocketry research and testing.

During World War I (1914–1918), the Germans launched solid-fuel rockets as weapons. When the war ended, a peace treaty called the Treaty of Versailles did not allow solid-fuel rocket research in Germany. But it did not specifically outlaw liquid-fuel rocket research.

The German army became interested in the VfR's work because it wanted to develop liquid-fuel rocket weapons. In 1932, the German Army Rocket Research Group was formed to research liquid-fuel rockets for the military. Do you think the German government was planning for another war?

Led by Wernher von Braun, the German rocket program created the V-2 rocket in 1944. The V-2 burned a mixture of liquid oxygen and alcohol. The V-2 was the world's first successful long-range **ballistic missile**. It could travel about 186 miles (300 kilometers) and carry a payload of about 2,205 pounds (1,000 kilograms). Germany fired thousands of V-2 rockets at Britain in 1944 and 1945 during World War II, killing many people and destroying much of London's infrastructure.

WORDS TO KNOW

ballistic missile: a missile that is at first powered and guided but is then pulled by gravity to its target.

guided missile: a self-propelled missile that can be steered in flight by remote control or by an onboard homing device.

OPERATION PAPERCLIP

At the end of World War II, both the United States and the Soviet Union realized the potential of rockets. Each country wanted the German scientists who held key knowledge about the superior Germany rocketry. Scientists who specialized in aerodynamics and rocketry and had been involved in the V-2 project were extremely valuable. Under the code name Operation Paperclip, U.S. intelligence agents and the military secretly brought German scientists and their families to the United States without State Department approval. Through Operation Paperclip, almost 500 German scientists moved to the United States. Most settled in New Mexico (White Sands Proving Ground), Texas (Fort Bliss), and Alabama (Huntsville), where they worked on **guided missile** and ballistic missile technology. About 60 V-2 rockets were also brought from Germany. The German scientists' expertise and the hardware from the German rockets helped the United States build the foundation of its rocketry and space travel programs.

After World War II, the United States and the Soviet Union realized that rockets could be powerful military weapons. Both countries used advances from the German rocketry program in their own rocket science programs. Many of the German scientists and engineers who had worked in the German rocketry programs moved to the United States or the Soviet Union and continued their research. Their knowledge helped both the Soviet Union and the United States develop rockets that could launch satellites and humans into space.

THE SPACE RACE

In the United States, teams of scientists and engineers experimented with ballistic rockets and missiles. Working at the Redstone Arsenal in Huntsville, Alabama, Wernher von Braun and his team created several kinds of medium- and long-range ballistic missiles. One of these missiles was the Redstone ballistic missile, which was based on technology from the German V-2 rocket.

Meanwhile, the Soviet Union was also developing its own powerful rockets with the help of V-2 documentation and German scientists. The Soviets created the R-7 rocket, a multi-stage, liquid-fuel rocket that could travel almost 7,500 miles

WORDS TO KNOW

artificial satellite: a manmade object that orbits around the earth or the moon.

(12,000 kilometers). On October 4, 1957, the Soviet Union used the R-7 to launch *Sputnik 1* into space. It was the first earth-orbiting **artificial satellite**. A month later, Soviet scientists launched a second satellite that carried a small dog named Laika into space.

THE WORLD WAS AMAZED AT THE SOVIET UNION'S ACHIEVEMENTS.

In the United States, rocket scientists hurried to catch up to the Soviets. They attempted to launch a satellite that was much smaller than *Sputnik*. On the launch day, December 6, 1957, the rocket lit and rose 2 feet (61 centimeters) above the launch pad. Then it sank back to the pad, fell over, and caught on fire. It was a complete failure.

Desperate for success, the United States turned to Wernher von Braun and his team at the Redstone Arsenal. Braun's team adapted the Redstone rocket so it could reach outer space. They added a fourth stage and renamed the rocket the Jupiter.

WHAT HAPPENED TO LAIKA?

How would living things survive in space? Scientists in the Soviet Union needed a way to test life-support systems for their satellite, *Sputnik 2*. They found a stray dog named Laika on the streets of Moscow and trained her for a space mission. Many people were outraged because the scientists knew that they were sending the little dog to her death. Laika survived the initial launch, but for years no one knew how she died.

Some people believed that she had **asphyxiated** when she ran out of oxygen. Other believed that the Soviets had **euthanized** her before she ran out of oxygen. In 2002, former Soviet scientist Dimitri Malashenkov told the World Space Congress that Laika had actually died within a few hours of achieving orbit. She died from stress and overheating because of an unreliable temperature control system.

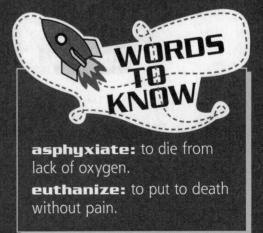

WORDS TO KNOW

asphyxiate: to die from lack of oxygen.
euthanize: to put to death without pain.

In January 1958, the Jupiter rocket launched successfully. It sent a satellite called *Explorer 1* into orbit around the earth.

Now that both countries had used rockets to send satellites into space, they entered the next phase of their fierce space race. Who could send a human into space? Who would reach the moon first?

WORDS TO KNOW

manned spacecraft: a spacecraft that carries humans.
cosmonaut: a Russian astronaut.

DID YOU KNOW?

In October 1958, the United States created the National Aeronautics and Space Administration (NASA). NASA's goal is the peaceful exploration of space for the benefit of humankind.

Scientists from both countries raced to develop a rocket that would be strong and powerful enough to lift a **manned spacecraft** into outer space.

In April 1961, a Russian rocket lifted **cosmonaut** Yuri Gagarin into space. He traveled once around the earth in an orbit that lasted 108 minutes. In May 1961, the United States launched a Redstone rocket that lifted American astronaut Alan Shepard and the *Freedom 7* spacecraft to 116 miles (187 kilometers) in altitude, not quite high enough to orbit the earth.

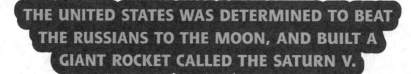

THE UNITED STATES WAS DETERMINED TO BEAT THE RUSSIANS TO THE MOON, AND BUILT A GIANT ROCKET CALLED THE SATURN V.

On July 16, 1969, *Apollo 11* launched from Cape Canaveral, Florida, powered by the Saturn V rocket. Astronauts Neil Armstrong and Edwin "Buzz" Aldrin became the first men to step on the moon's surface. Can you remember any famous first steps taken in your lifetime? What was the public's reaction?

Armstrong and Aldrin stayed on the moon for only a few hours to collect moon rocks and set up experiments. After this monumental moon landing, the Saturn V launched astronauts to the moon five more times. The Apollo program ended in 1972, and since then no one has been back to the moon.

THE SATURN V

The Saturn V is the largest and most powerful rocket built to date. It is the only rocket so far that has sent astronauts to the moon. The Saturn V was 363 feet (111 meters) tall, as tall as a 36-story building. It weighed 6.1 million pounds (272,155 metric tons). Equipped with three stages and 11 liquid-fuel rocket engines, it was first launched in 1967 and completed its last launch in 1973. The Saturn V could carry 285,000 pounds (129 metric tons) of payload into space to orbit the earth. Of the 15 Saturn V rockets made, 13 were launched into space, sending 12 astronauts to the moon.

PS You can watch a video of the very first moon landing. How do you think people in 1969 reacted to this footage? Do you think people react differently to scenes from space today?

Since the first primitive bamboo tubes, rockets have launched many people and machines into space. Astronauts have orbited the earth, landed on the moon, and built the International Space Station. Robot spacecraft have traveled to other planets to learn about them. Many countries have launched satellites into space for science, communication, and weather forecasting.

AS OUR KNOWLEDGE OF ROCKETRY INCREASES, THE UNIVERSE APPEARS LIMITLESS.

WORDS TO KNOW

universe: everything that exists everywhere.

AEOLIPILE

In this project, you can recreate the work of the Greek mathematician Hero, using water instead of steam. The basic **principle** of action and reaction is the same—for every action, there is an equal and opposite reaction. As the water shoots out of the holes in the carton, it pushes on the carton with an equal force. **NOTE: This project is best performed outside.**

1 Use the scissors to poke a hole near the bottom left corner of each side of the milk carton. Open up the carton at the top.

2 Punch a hole in the top of the carton and thread the string through the hole. You can hold the other end of the string to hang it over the tub or bucket, or tie it to something like a tree branch. The carton should be able to rotate freely.

WORDS TO KNOW

principle: the basic way that something works.

3 Seal the four holes with waterproof tape and fill the carton halfway with water.

4 Either hang the carton from the string or hold it over the tub. Quickly remove the tape and watch.

What's Happening? What is the water making the carton do? This is an example of the same force that makes rockets work! If you fill the carton with different amounts of water, how does that affect the carton's reaction?

— CHAPTER 2 —
BASIC ROCKET SCIENCE: NEWTON'S LAWS OF MOTION

In 1687, a scientist named Sir Isaac Newton published a document that detailed his three famous laws of motion. These laws are the foundation of all rocket science. Understanding Newton's laws and the basic science behind them will help you build and launch a successful rocket.

The first fire arrows used by the Chinese were very unpredictable. The rocket might fly high into the air. It might skip around close to the ground, shooting smoke and sparks. Other times, it might explode right at the launch area. Why was this a problem?

DURING SEVERAL CENTURIES, ROCKET LAUNCHERS USED TRIAL AND ERROR TO IMPROVE ROCKETS AND MAKE THEM MORE RELIABLE.

SIR ISAAC NEWTON

Born on January 4, 1643, in Woolsthorpe, England, Isaac Newton was the only son of a local farmer. His father had died a few months before his birth and Newton was raised by his grandparents. In 1661, he attended Cambridge University. There he studied mathematics, **optics**, physics, and **astronomy**.

When a **plague** outbreak forced the university to close in October 1665, Newton returned home to Woolsthorpe for two years. During that time, he experimented with gravity, optics, and mathematics. In 1667, Newton returned to Cambridge. He became a fellow of Trinity College and, later, a professor of mathematics. Through the years, Newton conducted many experiments and published papers on light, history, **theology**, and **alchemy**.

Newton published his most famous work, *Philosophiae Naturalis Principia Mathematica (Mathematical Principles of Natural Philosophy)*, in 1687. In this work, Newton stated his three laws of motion. These clear statements of the laws laid the foundation for rocketry as a science. Using these laws, scientists had a better understanding of how rockets launched and moved.

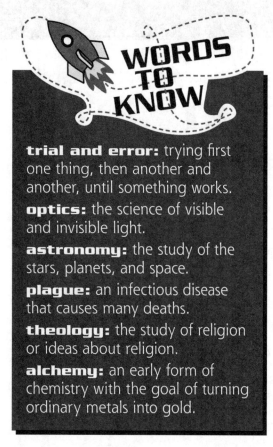

WORDS TO KNOW

trial and error: trying first one thing, then another and another, until something works.

optics: the science of visible and invisible light.

astronomy: the study of the stars, planets, and space.

plague: an infectious disease that causes many deaths.

theology: the study of religion or ideas about religion.

alchemy: an early form of chemistry with the goal of turning ordinary metals into gold.

FIRST LAW OF MOTION: LAW OF INERTIA

Newton's first law of motion states that an object at rest stays at rest and an object in motion stays in motion with the same speed and in the same direction, unless it is acted upon by an **unbalanced force**. This law is based on the principle of **inertia**.

To understand what Newton meant by this law, you first need to understand the terms *rest*, *motion*, and *unbalanced force*.

> **WHEN AN OBJECT IS STILL AND NOT MOVING, IT IS SAID TO BE AT REST.**

You are at rest while sitting in a chair. However, even though you are not moving, there are forces acting on you. The force of gravity is trying to pull you downward. At the same time, your chair is pushing you up. The two forces are equal and balanced, which allows you to sit on the chair.

WORDS TO KNOW

unbalanced force: a force that has no partner force of equal power acting on it in the opposite direction.

inertia: the tendency of matter to either stay at rest or stay in motion unless acted upon by a force.

If someone pulls your chair out from under you, however, the forces acting on you become unbalanced. The force of gravity pulling you down becomes stronger than any forces holding you up. You move from resting to motion as you fall to the floor!

Gravity Pushes Down

Chair Pushes Up

When applied to rockets, Newton's first law simply says that when a rocket is at rest upon a launch pad, it will need the push of an unbalanced force to cause it to move and launch. That force is called thrust, and it is produced by the rocket's engines. In order for the rocket to move, thrust must be greater than the force of gravity holding the rocket on the ground.

WORDS TO KNOW

exhaust gases: the hot gases produced from a rocket's engine.

pressure: the force that pushes on an object.

nozzle: a narrow opening at the base of a rocket that controls the flow of exhaust gases from its engine.

If thrust's upward push is greater than gravity's downward pull, the forces acting on the rocket will become unbalanced. The rocket will shoot into the air. As long as the rocket's engine produces a thrust force, the rocket accelerates in flight.

When the engines burn out, the forces acting upon the rocket become unbalanced again. Gravity becomes stronger and pulls the rocket back to Earth. When the rocket lands on the ground, the rocket is at rest again. The forces acting on it are in balance once again.

COMBUSTION

The hot gases that push a rocket off the launch pad come from combustion. In a rocket, combustion occurs inside a hollow area called the combustion chamber. Combustion produces hot gases called **exhaust gases**. These gases expand very quickly and **pressure** builds inside the combustion chamber. The gases have only one way to get out—through the rocket's exhaust **nozzle**. When they shoot out of the rocket's nozzle, the gases create a pushing force called thrust.

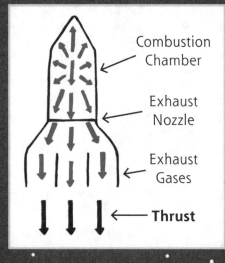

Combustion Chamber

Exhaust Nozzle

Exhaust Gases

Thrust

IN ROCKETRY, FORCES FREQUENTLY MOVE FROM BALANCED TO UNBALANCED AND BACK AGAIN.

WORDS TO KNOW

metric: relating to or using the metric system of measurement, which is based on units of 10.

net force: a force that is the result of two or more forces acting together.

When a spacecraft reaches outer space, it is no longer affected by the pull of gravity. Even so, it will still react to other forces. If the forces acting on a rocket are in balance, the spacecraft will travel in a straight line through space. It will only change its motion if acted upon by an unbalanced force. If the spacecraft flies close to a large body such as Earth, another planet, or the moon, the gravity of that body will pull on the craft. This unbalances the forces acting on the craft and changes its path.

DID YOU KNOW?

The quantity of force is measured by a standard **metric** unit called the "newton."

SECOND LAW OF MOTION: LAW OF ACCELERATION

Newton's second law of motion explains how objects behave when there are unbalanced forces. Acceleration is a change in motion—speeding up, slowing down, or changing direction. The acceleration of an object depends on two things: the **net force** acting on the object and the mass of the object.

The law states that the acceleration of an object depends directly on the size of the force acting on it. If the size of the force acting on an object increases, the object's acceleration will also increase.

The second factor that affects an object's acceleration is the object's mass. The greater an object's mass, the less acceleration it will have. Think about it like this—if you use the same amount of force to push a small rock or a heavy boulder, which one do you think will move faster? Which one has less mass and, therefore, more acceleration?

OUCH!

F = MA

Newton's second law is often explained by the mathematical formula f=ma, which stands for force = mass x acceleration. For rockets, the parts of the equation can be thought of as follows:

- f = force or thrust produced by a rocket engine
- m = mass of the gas and particles produced by the burning rocket propellant
- a = acceleration of these products out of the back of the engine as exhaust

The more propellant burned and the greater the acceleration of the exhaust, the greater the thrust created to launch the rocket. In other words, to generate a large force to propel the rocket, the engine must burn a large mass of fuel and push the gas exhaust out of the engine as quickly as possible.

A rocket's fuel is a large part of its total mass. As the fuel burns and is used up, the rocket's mass decreases. As a result, the thrust force has less mass to push, so it can push the rocket faster. As the rocket gets lighter, the rocket speeds up.

THIRD LAW OF MOTION: LAW OF REACTION

Newton's third law of motion states that every action has an equal and opposite reaction. You've probably heard this before, because it is the most well known of Newton's laws of motion. But what does it mean?

To understand Newton's third law of motion, think about a diving board. When you stand on the end of the board, your feet **exert** a downward force on the board. At the same time, the board is exerting an upward force on you. Otherwise, it would collapse and send you falling into the pool. These two forces act together as a pair and are balanced. One force meets another force in the opposite direction. To jump from the diving board, you push down on the board and create an unbalanced force. The board's reaction force pushes back on you and propels you off the board and into the pool.

exert: to make an intense action or effort.

Balanced Forces

You Push Down

Board Pushes Back

LIFT OFF!

Another way to think about the principle of action and reaction is to picture a skateboard. When a rider jumps on a skateboard and pushes off the ground, it is an action. This action has an equal and opposite reaction and the skateboard rolls in the opposite direction.

ROCKETRY

When a rocket lifts off the ground, it also follows the principle of action and reaction. The rocket pushes hot exhaust gas in one direction—the action. This action pushes the rocket in the opposite direction—the reaction. The more force a rocket generates when pushing out the gas, the more force it will have to launch a rocket all the way into space. In order for the rocket to leave the ground, thrust must be greater than the rocket's weight.

THE MORE WEIGHT A ROCKET CARRIES, THE GREATER THE THRUST NEEDED TO LAUNCH IT.

GALILEO'S WORK

An Italian scientist named Galileo Galilei, who died the year before Sir Isaac Newton was born, studied physics and motion. Through many experiments, Galileo concluded that moving objects did not need continuous application of force to keep moving. Galileo also developed the principle of inertia. Because of inertia, all matter resists changes in motion. If an object is in motion, it remains in motion unless an **opposing force** such as **friction** acts to slow it down. The more mass an object has, the more it resists changes in motion. Newton studied Galileo's work on inertia when developing his laws of motion.

WORDS TO KNOW

opposing force: a force that acts in a pair against another force.
friction: a force that slows down objects when they rub against each other.

28

PUTTING IT ALL TOGETHER

Newton's laws of motion are the basic scientific principles that explain much of how rockets work.

Newton's first law: An object will remain at rest or at a constant velocity unless an external force acts upon it. An unbalanced force is needed to move a rocket from rest into motion.

Newton's second law: An object's velocity will change when an external force acts upon it. The amount of force or thrust produced by the rocket's engine is determined by the mass of the exhaust and the speed with which it leaves the engine.

Newton's third law: Every action has an equal and opposite reaction. The thrust from the engine is the action that creates an equal reaction in the rocket and sends it flying in the opposite direction.

NEWTON'S THIRD LAW IN SPACE

How can rockets work in space where there is no air for them to push against? Actually, when a rocket moves through air, the air resistance causes a friction force called **drag**. Drag pushes in the opposite direction of the rocket's movement. It causes the rocket to slow down. As a result, more thrust is needed to move the rocket through air. Space is a vacuum, so when gas leaves the rocket's engine, there is no air to create drag and slow it down. Therefore, less thrust is needed to move the rocket in space. This is what Robert Goddard proved when he launched a rocket inside his airless chamber and discovered the rocket had 20 percent more thrust.

WORDS TO KNOW

drag: the resistance air exerts on a body moving through it.

You can read Newton's notebooks for yourself. Does seeing his handwriting make you think differently about his work?

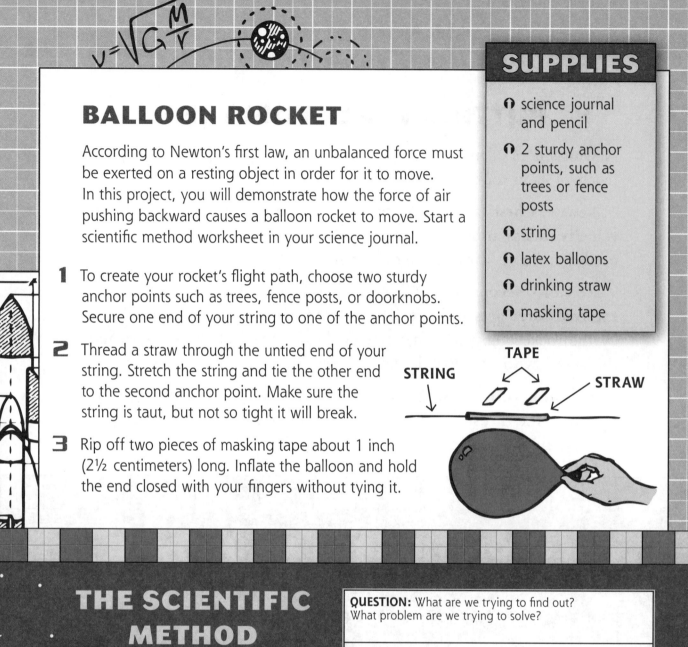

$$v=\sqrt{G\frac{M}{r}}$$

BALLOON ROCKET

According to Newton's first law, an unbalanced force must be exerted on a resting object in order for it to move. In this project, you will demonstrate how the force of air pushing backward causes a balloon rocket to move. Start a scientific method worksheet in your science journal.

1 To create your rocket's flight path, choose two sturdy anchor points such as trees, fence posts, or doorknobs. Secure one end of your string to one of the anchor points.

2 Thread a straw through the untied end of your string. Stretch the string and tie the other end to the second anchor point. Make sure the string is taut, but not so tight it will break.

3 Rip off two pieces of masking tape about 1 inch (2½ centimeters) long. Inflate the balloon and hold the end closed with your fingers without tying it.

SUPPLIES

- science journal and pencil
- 2 sturdy anchor points, such as trees or fence posts
- string
- latex balloons
- drinking straw
- masking tape

STRING **TAPE** **STRAW**

THE SCIENTIFIC METHOD

Every good scientist keeps a science journal! Scientists use the scientific method to keep their experiments organized.

Choose a notebook to use as your science journal and record each step in the scientific method worksheet, like the one shown here.

QUESTION: What are we trying to find out? What problem are we trying to solve?
RESEARCH: What do other people think?
HYPOTHESIS/PREDICTION: What do we think the answer will be?
EQUIPMENT: What supplies are we using?
METHOD: What procedure are we following?
RESULTS: What happened and why?

$$\frac{v^2}{r} = g$$

4 While still holding the balloon's end closed with one hand, attach the inflated balloon to the straw, using the two pieces of masking tape. Make sure that the end of the balloon is pointing away from the direction it is going to move.

5 Release the balloon and watch it take off! As the air is released in one direction, the balloon travels in the opposite direction.

6 Repeat the demonstration with another balloon. This time, measure how far the balloon travels on the string. Vary the amount of air in the balloon. How does this affect the distance the balloon rocket travels? Does the balloon spin around the string as it moves? If so, what do you think causes the spinning motion? Which of Newton's laws is being demonstrated by the balloon?

7 Record your observations in your scientific method worksheet. You can write your measurements on a chart like this:

	LOW AIR	MEDIUM AIR	LOTS OF AIR
Distance Traveled			
Time			

Try This: Adjust your string so that the rocket travels a vertical flight path, like a space shuttle launch. What happens when you launch the balloon? How far does it travel? How does that compare to a similarly inflated balloon traveling a horizontal flight path? Can you explain the difference?

$$v = \sqrt{G\frac{M}{r}}$$

ROCKET EXHAUST

SUPPLIES

- science journal and pencil
- flight path from the Balloon Rocket project on page 30
- masking tape
- latex balloons
- funnel
- flour

A rocket at rest moves when force is applied to it. In the case of a balloon rocket, air leaving the balloon creates a force that sets the balloon into motion. Because air is invisible, you cannot see it leaving the balloon. Using flour, you can create an exhaust trail from your balloon rocket and see the force of air leaving the balloon. Start a scientific method worksheet in your science journal. **NOTE: This project is best performed outside.**

1 Reuse the flight path created in the Balloon Rocket project on page 30.

2 Rip off two pieces of masking tape about 1 inch (2½ centimeters) long and put aside for later.

3 Use the funnel to pour some flour into an uninflated balloon.

4 Inflate the balloon and pinch its neck closed with your fingers. Keeping the neck pinched shut, attached the balloon to the straw using the two pieces of masking tape.

5 Gently shake the balloon to loosen the flour inside and then quickly release it. Can you see the rocket exhaust? What does it look like? How does it behave?

Try This: Use different amounts of flour and different levels of inflation to make more balloon rockets. How do these changes affect the rockets' exhaust? Why do you think this happens?

$$\frac{v^2}{r} = g$$

CREATE A ROCKET-POWERED BOAT

You can use air to create thrust that will power a boat. Start a scientific method worksheet in your science journal.

1 Using the scissors, cut off one long side of the carton, so that a three-sided box remains.

2 Use the scissors to make a hole approximately ½ inch (1¼ centimeter) in diameter in the bottom of the carton.

3 Blow up the balloon and hold the neck closed.

4 Place the inflated balloon into the carton boat. Pull the balloon neck out through the hole in the bottom of the carton, making sure that you keep it pinched shut the entire time so that no air escapes the balloon.

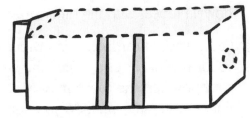

5 While still holding the balloon's neck closed, place the boat carrying the balloon into the water.

6 Release the end of the balloon. What happens? In which direction does the air flowing out of the balloon cause the boat to move—in the same or in the opposite direction?

Try This: Repeat the experiment with a different-sized balloon or carton. How does that affect the distance your boat travels? You can also try adding weight to the bottom of the boat. Does that make the boat move faster or slower?

$$v = \sqrt{G\frac{M}{r}}$$

BALLOON-ROCKET CAR

Using rocket power, you can design your own model car. A scientific method worksheet will help keep you organized. **Caution: Have an adult help with the hot glue.**

SUPPLIES

- science journal and pencil
- 4 wheels or plastic bottle caps of the same size
- hot glue gun
- 2 thin wooden dowels or skewers
- drinking straws
- scissors
- cardboard
- masking tape
- balloons
- rubber band

1 Glue a wheel to one end of each wooden dowel. Allow the glue to dry completely before moving to the next step.

2 Cut two pieces of straw, each a little shorter than the dowels from step 1. Thread a dowel through one straw and hot glue the second wheel to the other end of the dowel. Repeat with the other straw and dowel.

3 Cut a piece of cardboard, no wider than your straw pieces, to form your car body. Tape the wheel assemblies to the car body. Test the car to make sure it rolls in a straight line. If it doesn't, what do you need to adjust to make it roll straight?

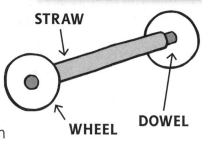

STRAW

WHEEL   DOWEL

4 Put a new straw through the balloon's opening and secure it with a rubber band. Using masking tape, secure the straw to the car's base. You may need to tape two or more straws together. Make sure the balloon faces forward and the end of the straw faces the rear of the car.

5 Blow into the straw and inflate the balloon. Hold your finger over the end of the straw to keep the air in the balloon as you place the car on the floor. Let go and watch the balloon power your car! What is making your car move?

6 Measure how far your car travels. Then see what design changes you can make to the car or its balloon rocket engine that will improve its performance.

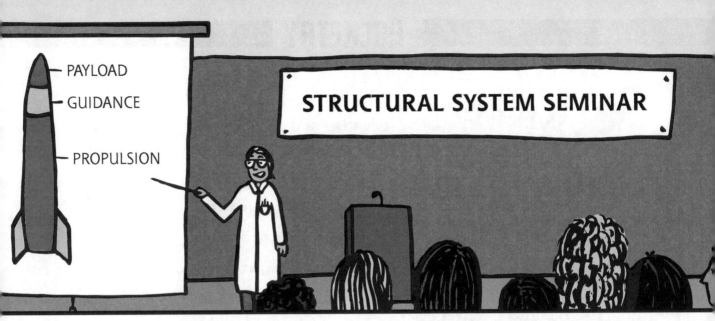

— CHAPTER 3 —
ROCKET DESIGN AND CONSTRUCTION

There are many different types of rockets. There are small rockets and large rockets, rockets that have been used for war, and rockets that have been used for science. Some rockets have launched only a few feet into the air, while others have blasted into outer space. All of these rockets have a few common **components** that help a rocket launch, fly, and land.

It's essential for every future rocket builder to learn the **terminology** and purpose of these components. Knowing how a rocket is built can help you understand how it launches and flies.

WORDS TO KNOW

component: an important part of a system or mixture.

terminology: the important words used in a specific subject.

To analyze and design rockets, scientists and engineers group parts with the same function into a system. **There are four major systems in a rocket:**

- **structural system;**
- **payload system;**
- **guidance system;** and
- **propulsion system.**

STRUCTURAL SYSTEM

A rocket's structural system includes its frame, body, and control fins. The main component of this system is the rocket body, which is called the **fuselage**. The fuselage is made from very strong materials such as titanium or aluminum.

Because the rocket's performance in flight depends on its weight and mass, the fuselage has to be very lightweight. The fuselage stores the rocket's fuel and fuel pumps and contains chambers where the fuel is ignited. Often the rocket's fuselage and other structural parts are coated with a **thermal** protection. This prevents the fuselage from melting from the heat created by the rocket's engine or from heat created by air friction during flight.

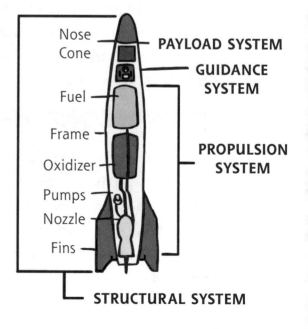

Nose Cone — **PAYLOAD SYSTEM**
GUIDANCE SYSTEM
Fuel
Frame
PROPULSION SYSTEM
Oxidizer
Pumps
Nozzle
Fins
STRUCTURAL SYSTEM

Another part of the rocket's structural system is the nozzle. A rocket's nozzle controls the flow of exhaust gases from its engine and is similar to the end of a balloon. If the end of the balloon is open, the balloon's air will escape, sending the balloon flying around the room. In the same way, when hot gases escape the rocket's nozzle, thrust sends the rocket into flight.

DID YOU KNOW?

Liquid-fuel rockets can generate more thrust than solid-fuel rockets. Yet they take longer to build up to maximum thrust, so they are not as powerful at the initial launch.

REMEMBER THE PROJECTS WHERE YOU ATTACHED THE BALLOON TO THE CAR, BOAT, AND STRAW? YOU WERE DEMONSTRATING WHAT HAPPENS WHEN YOU CREATE THRUST.

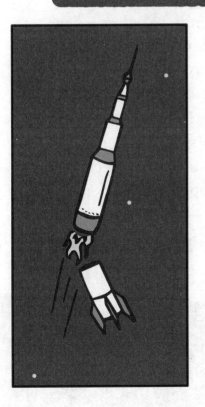

During a rocket's flight, some parts of the structural system may be discarded. In a multi-stage rocket, engineers stack several small rockets, or stages, on top of a larger rocket, which is the first stage. Each stage has its own propellant, engines, instruments, and frame.

The first stage is powerful enough to lift its own mass and the mass of the other stages. When the first stage burns through its propellant and is empty, it simply drops off. The second stage fires, then the third stage. Every time one of the rocket's stages drops off, the rocket's total mass decreases. This allows the second and third stages to operate more efficiently.

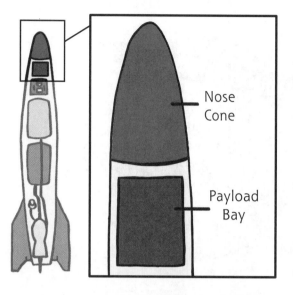

Nose Cone

Payload Bay

PAYLOAD SYSTEM

A payload is something a rocket carries. The payload system in a rocket depends on the rocket's purpose, but can include astronauts, scientific equipment, spacecraft, or weapons. Some of the earliest payloads were fireworks. During World War II, the German V-2 rockets carried payloads of several thousand pounds of explosives. Other rockets have carried satellites into space. What are satellites used for? Why are they important?

A rocket's payload can also be a human being. Rockets have launched manned spacecraft into orbit to explore, conduct scientific experiments, and to carry materials and crews to and from space stations. The payload is usually protected in a nose cone at the top of the rocket.

DID YOU KNOW?

The Hubble Space Telescope is an example of a rocket payload that has been used for exploring deep space. Without rockets, we may never have been able to see this far away.

PS

You can see pictures taken by the Hubble Space Telescope.

GUIDANCE SYSTEM

A rocket's guidance system includes all of the computers, sensors, **radar**, and other equipment necessary to control the rocket once it is in flight. The guidance system keeps the rocket **stable** in flight. It also helps to steer the rocket.

WORDS TO KNOW

radar: a device that detects objects by bouncing radio waves off them and measuring how long it takes for the waves to return.

stable: reliable and steady.

A rocket's flight is determined by the forces acting on the rocket. By understanding how these forces affect a rocket's motion, engineers can design different guidance systems that control the rocket in flight.

Small rockets generally only need stabilizing controls. A fin fixed to the rocket's body is a simple way to **stabilize** it. A larger rocket may need a guidance system that stabilizes it and also allows it to change direction. It may use a special type of nozzle called a **gimbaled nozzle**. Many modern rockets use a gimbaled nozzle. The gimbal can swivel from side to side, changing the direction of the rocket's thrust and, as a result, changing the direction of the rocket.

WORDS TO KNOW

stabilize: to make reliable and steady.

gimbaled nozzle: a nozzle that can swivel from side to side, changing the direction of the engine's thrust to adjust its flight path.

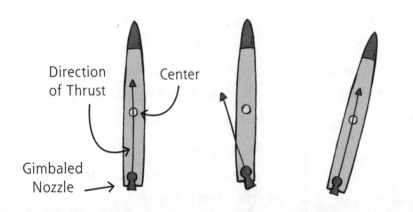

Direction of Thrust

Center

Gimbaled Nozzle

ROCKET VS. GUIDED MISSILE

A rocket and a guided missile are not the same thing. Rockets don't have guidance systems. A rocket must be fired in the direction it needs to go. A guided missile has a guidance system that tells it where to go. As a military weapon, a guided missile's payload is a warhead, such as the V-2s used by Germany in World War II.

PROPULSION SYSTEM

Today, most rockets are propelled by forcing a gas from the rear of the engine at a very high speed. The parts needed to propel a rocket, including the rocket engine, tanks, pumps, propellants, power head, and rocket nozzle, are part of its propulsion system. The primary purpose of the propulsion system is to produce thrust, the force that launches a rocket and moves it through air and space.

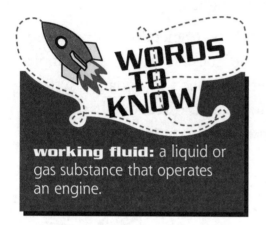

WORDS TO KNOW

working fluid: a liquid or gas substance that operates an engine.

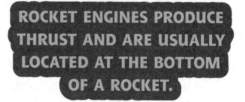

ROCKET ENGINES PRODUCE THRUST AND ARE USUALLY LOCATED AT THE BOTTOM OF A ROCKET.

Thrust can be generated in different ways, using different propulsion systems. All propulsion systems, however, use some sort of **working fluid**, which is accelerated by the system. The reaction to this acceleration creates a force on the system.

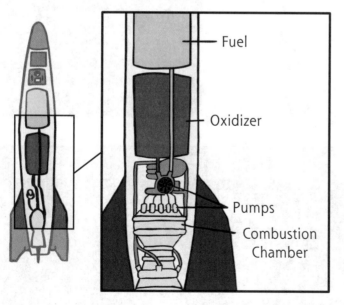

Fuel

Oxidizer

Pumps

Combustion Chamber

Remember the balloons you used for the projects in the last chapter? In a balloon, the working fluid is air. When the air is released and accelerated through the balloon's end, it creates a force that propels the balloon around the room.

In a rocket's propulsion system, a fuel and an oxidizer are mixed. The mixture causes a chemical reaction in a combustion chamber, which in turn produces a gas of hot exhaust.

THE HOT EXHAUST IS THE ROCKET'S WORKING FLUID.

As the hot exhaust builds up in the chamber, it passes through a nozzle, which accelerates its flow outward. As the hot exhaust passes through the nozzle, it creates thrust to propel the rocket. When the main rocket engine cannot provide enough thrust, sometimes booster rockets are attached to provide extra thrust during launch.

DID YOU KNOW?

A rocket is called a reaction engine because it works on the principle of action and reaction.

ROCKET FUEL

A rocket's propulsion system will depend on the type of fuel that it uses. If the rocket uses a solid propellant, the propellants are mixed together and packed into a solid cylinder. The solid propellant is ignited when exposed to a heat source from an igniter. Once it begins to burn, a solid propellant will continue to burn until all of the propellant has been used.

In rockets that use a liquid propellant, the fuel and the oxidizer are stored separately in tanks as liquids. When thrust is needed, the propellants are pumped into a combustion chamber where they will burn. With a liquid propulsion system, you can stop burning and as a result stop thrust by simply turning off the flow of propellants into the combustion chamber. Because they need more equipment, such as high-capacity pumps and storage tanks, liquid propulsions systems are usually heavier and more complex than solid propulsion systems. The German V-2 rocket used a liquid propulsion system, carrying propellant tanks, pumps, a combustion chamber, and nozzle.

STRING ROCKET

A rocket's propulsion system generates thrust that propels the rocket. In this project, you will test how different pressure levels affect thrust. Start a scientific method worksheet in your science journal. **Note: You may need an adult's help for certain portions of this activity. All participants should use safety glasses.**

1 Put on your safety glasses. With an adult's help, drill a hole in the lid of your plastic bottle. Make the hole small enough so that it just fits the inflating needle. You may want to use a vise to hold the lid while drilling.

2 Make a test range that is at least 50 feet (15 meters) long by securing one of your strings to an immovable object such as a tree or fence. Thread a straw through the string. Then secure the string's other end to a second immovable object. Make sure the string is taut.

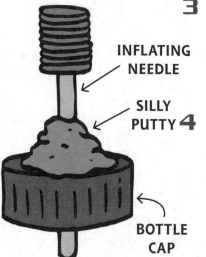

INFLATING NEEDLE

SILLY PUTTY

BOTTLE CAP

3 Replace the cap on the bottle rocket and tape the bottle to the straw on the string. Make sure the cap is pointed away from the string's path.

4 To add pressure to the bottle, mold some Silly Putty around the base of the inflating needle. Attach the needle to the bike pump's hose and insert the needle into the drill hole in the top of the bottle cap. Press the Silly Putty around the hole to seal it.

AIR-POWERED ROCKET LAUNCHER

An air-powered rocket uses a blast of rapidly expanding air to propel it upward. A pump forces air into a PVC tube, which launches the rocket into the air. You can build your own air launcher with a few common items from the hardware store. **Caution: Because this activity involves the use of several tools, ask an adult to help you. Be sure to wear safety glasses when launching rockets.**

1 Have an adult cut the PVC pipe into the necessary pieces. You may be able to ask your local hardware store to cut the pipe for you.

2 Place the four-way fitting on the ground. Insert the two 12-inch (30-centimeter) pieces of PVC into opposite sides of the four-way fitting that point east and west. Insert the 40-inch (1-meter) piece pointing north. Insert the 5-inch (13-centimeter) piece pointing south.

- ½-inch PVC pipe cut to lengths:
  - ➲ 40 inches (1 meter)
  - ➲ 18 inches (45 centimeters)
  - ➲ 5 inches (13 centimeters)
  - ➲ 2, 12 inches (30 centimeters)
- ½-inch, 90-degree PVC elbow
- ½-inch PVC four-way fitting
- ½-inch PVC end caps (2)
- 1-inch PVC coupling
- 1-inch by ½-inch PVC bushing
- PVC cement
- 2-liter bottle cap
- drill
- hot glue gun and glue
- several 2-liter soda bottles
- safety glasses

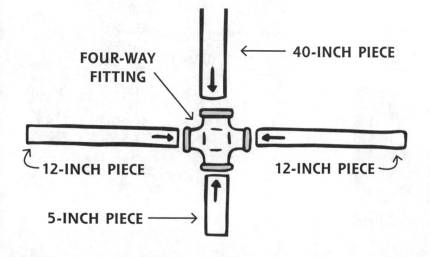

FOUR-WAY FITTING

← 40-INCH PIECE

12-INCH PIECE

12-INCH PIECE

5-INCH PIECE →

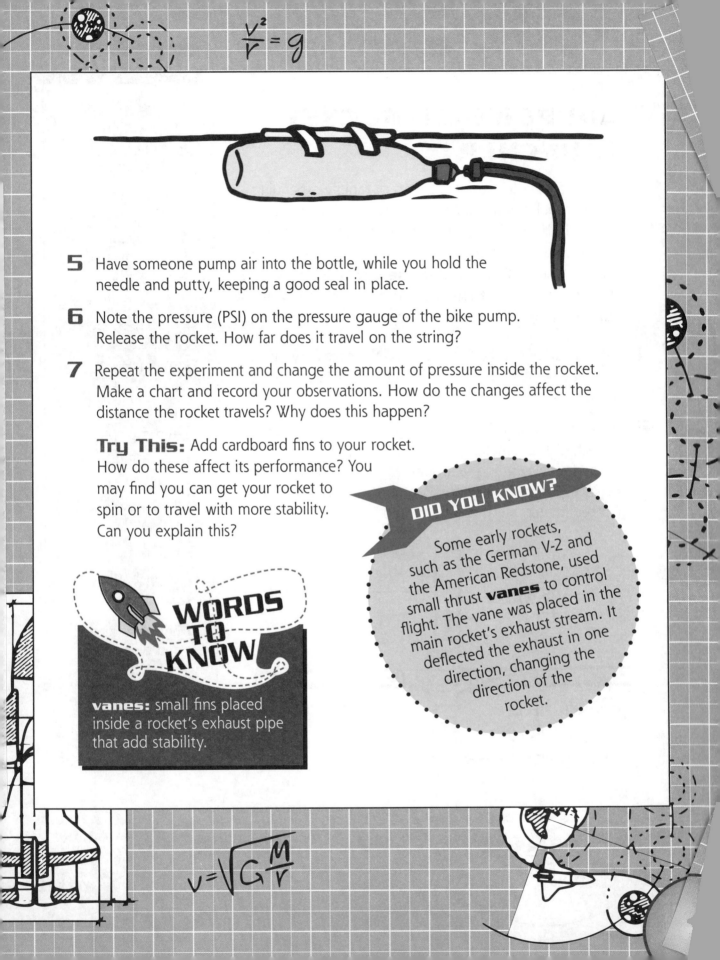

$$\frac{v^2}{r} = g$$

5 Have someone pump air into the bottle, while you hold the needle and putty, keeping a good seal in place.

6 Note the pressure (PSI) on the pressure gauge of the bike pump. Release the rocket. How far does it travel on the string?

7 Repeat the experiment and change the amount of pressure inside the rocket. Make a chart and record your observations. How do the changes affect the distance the rocket travels? Why does this happen?

Try This: Add cardboard fins to your rocket. How do these affect its performance? You may find you can get your rocket to spin or to travel with more stability. Can you explain this?

WORDS TO KNOW

vanes: small fins placed inside a rocket's exhaust pipe that add stability.

DID YOU KNOW?

Some early rockets, such as the German V-2 and the American Redstone, used small thrust **vanes** to control flight. The vane was placed in the main rocket's exhaust stream. It deflected the exhaust in one direction, changing the direction of the rocket.

$$v = \sqrt{G\frac{M}{r}}$$

$$\frac{v^2}{r} = g$$

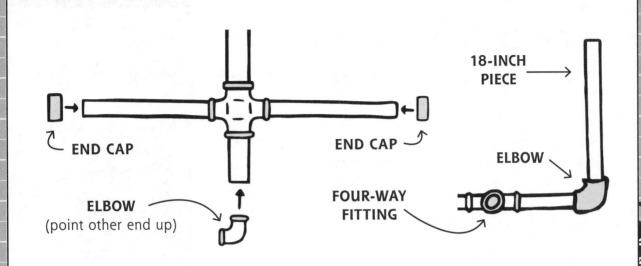

18-INCH PIECE

END CAP

END CAP

ELBOW

ELBOW
(point other end up)

FOUR-WAY FITTING

3 Place the end caps on the open ends of the 12-inch (30 centimeters) pieces. Place the 90-degree elbow on the open end of the 5-inch (13-centimeter) piece, so that it is pointing up. Fit the 18-inch (45-centimeter) piece into the vertical end of the elbow.

4 The coupling and the bushing fit together at the open end of the longest, 40-inch (1-meter) piece.

5 Glue all the pieces together using PVC cement and let it dry.

6 Have an adult drill holes through the center of the bottle cap and glue it inside the end of the coupling.

7 After the glue has set, attach an empty 2-liter soda bottle to the end of the launcher by screwing it into the glued-on cap. Your launcher is ready for action!

$$v = \sqrt{G\frac{M}{r}}$$

ROCKET NOSE CONE

A force called drag acts on a rocket when it flies through the air. Drag is an aerodynamic force that opposes the movement of an object through the air. It is a type of friction between the object's surface and the air it travels through. In this experiment, you will investigate how engineers design a rocket's nose cone to reduce the amount of drag that acts on a rocket in flight. Start a scientific method worksheet in your science journal.

1 Design at least three different nose cone shapes and cut them out of cardstock. Try a simple cutout that lies flat against the end of the paper towel tube and different cone shapes.

2 Attach a piece of clay to the nose cone to provide mass. Make sure you use the same amount of clay for each rocket, so that they have the same mass.

3 Tape your nose cone to a paper towel tube. Repeat for the different nose cone designs.

4 **Put on your safety glasses.** Using the air-powered rocket launcher, launch each rocket straight up. Record your observations about its flight. Which nose cone design produces the best performance?

Try This: Angle the launcher so that the rocket launches at an approximately 45-degree angle. Make sure it is not pointing toward any people or objects! Launch a rocket and use a tape measure or yard stick to measure the distance it travels. Repeat for each nose cone design. Which nose cone design allows the rocket to travel the farthest distance?

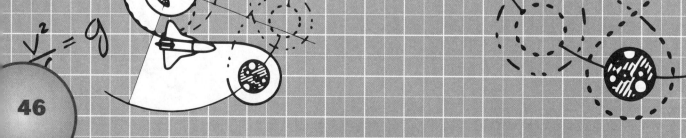

$$\frac{v^2}{r} = g$$

SUPPLIES

- science journal and pencil
- paper
- scissors
- tape
- index cards
- drinking straw

STRAW ROCKET

As a rocket flies, air pushes against it and slows it down. Drag is caused by friction between the air and the rocket's surface. A rocket's shape affects the amount of drag it experiences. In this project, you will design straw rockets and test how different designs affect performance. Start a scientific method worksheet in your science journal.

1 Cut out a long rectangle from your paper. Tightly roll the paper lengthwise around a pencil and tape it securely so that it forms a tube. Remove the pencil.

2 Cut out four fins from index cards and tape them to the rocket body. Place the straw inside the rocket, lining up the front of the rocket with the straw's end. Tape the end of the rocket closed.

3 To launch, go outside and blow into the straw. How does your rocket fly? Record your observations.

4 Build more straw rockets with new and different fin shapes and placement. You can also twist the end of your rocket closed to form a nose cone. Which design allows the rocket to fly the farthest?

WORDS TO KNOW

atmosphere: the blanket of air surrounding the earth.

DID YOU KNOW?

Rockets are the only engines that work in space. Jets and other engines need oxygen from the **atmosphere** to operate. Rockets carry their own oxygen.

$$v = \sqrt{G\frac{M}{r}}$$

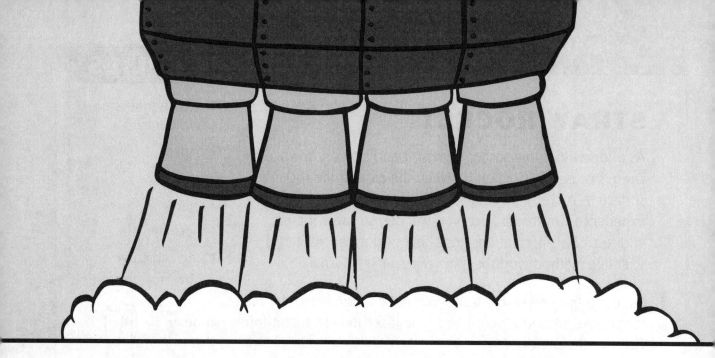

— CHAPTER 4 —
TAKING OFF: LAUNCH!

So how do rockets launch from the ground into the air, and sometimes into orbit? Whether it is a Chinese fire arrow or a sophisticated space shuttle, all rockets operate under the same laws of physics and motion. For every rocket, the launch is a mighty battle between forces.

BATTLE FORCE: GRAVITY

When a rocket sits at rest on a launch pad, the force of gravity pulls down on it. Gravity holds the rocket on the earth, the same way it holds you on the earth. Gravity is a force that pulls two objects together. In this case, it pulls the rocket and the earth together. The more mass an object has, the stronger the gravity force acting on it. That explains why objects with a large mass, such as a rocket, are very heavy.

Even though gravity is pulling down on the rocket, it does not sink into the dirt. An opposing force from the launch pad pushes upward on the bottom of the rocket against gravity. The two opposing forces are in balance, and the rocket remains at rest on the launch pad. This demonstrates Newton's first law of motion, that an object at rest will stay at rest.

DID YOU KNOW?

Most of a rocket's power is needed at the beginning of a launch. Lifting the weight of the rocket and its load of fuel takes a lot of power.

ITS OPPONENT: THRUST

In order to move the rocket and launch it from the ground, an unbalanced force must push on it. This force is called thrust, which pushes against gravity. If thrust wins the battle, it pushes the rocket off the launch pad and moves it through air and space. When the rocket is sitting upright, thrust pushes against the ground. Think about it this way: when you are about to jump into the air, you push your leg muscles into the ground. The force of your muscles pushing propels you into the air. In the same way, a rocket's engine creates thrust, which pushes out the bottom of the rocket.

THE FORCES OF THRUST AND GRAVITY BATTLE AGAINST EACH OTHER.

Thrust pushes up, while gravity pulls down on the rocket. If thrust's upward push is greater than gravity's downward pull, the forces acting on the rocket become unbalanced. One is stronger than the other. Following Newton's first law, the rocket shoots into the air.

49

LAUNCH TRAGEDY: THE *CHALLENGER* EXPLODES

Launch is the most dangerous part of a space mission. The rocket carries a full load of fuel and can blow up accidentally. In 1986, the space shuttle *Challenger* launched carrying a crew of seven astronauts. One of the crew, Christa McAuliffe, was on board as the first teacher in space. With the world watching the launch on television broadcasts, *Challenger* exploded within 73 seconds of takeoff.

An investigation revealed the *Challenger* explosion was caused by weather conditions. Low temperatures on the day of the launch kept an O-ring in the right solid rocket booster from sealing properly. Hot gases from the booster escaped, burning the booster, the external tank, and the orbiter. The orbiter exploded into fragments. After the disaster, NASA halted the space shuttle program for 32 months. Can you think of more recent tragedies that have interrupted scientific progress?

DID YOU KNOW?

Rockets have been designed and launched with up to five stages, but most rockets use two or three stages.

TO PROVIDE THE THRUST A ROCKET NEEDS TO LAUNCH, A ROCKET NEEDS PROPELLANT.

A rocket's propulsion system creates the thrust needed to launch. Rockets generally produce thrust by burning propellants. A propellant is a combination of fuel and an oxidizer, which provides the oxygen needed for the fuel to burn. Different types of propellants are used in different rockets. Some rockets, such as the space shuttle, even use more than one type of propellant.

Most rocket propellants are either solid or liquid based. When the propellant burns quickly, it releases hot, expanding gases called **combustion products** or exhaust. The rocket shoots the combustion products out of the rocket's engine, which creates thrust and launches the rocket.

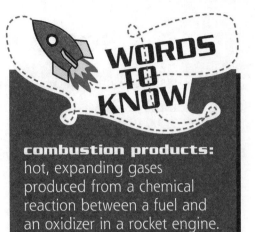

WORDS TO KNOW

combustion products: hot, expanding gases produced from a chemical reaction between a fuel and an oxidizer in a rocket engine.

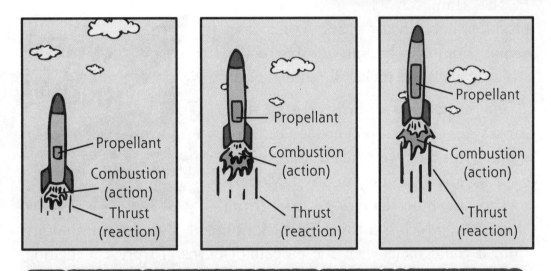

THE AMOUNT OF THRUST PRODUCED BY THE ROCKET DEPENDS ON HOW FAST THE COMBUSTION PRODUCTS LEAVE THE ENGINE.

This follows Newton's second law, which states that the force produced by the rocket's engine is a product of the mass of the exhaust and the acceleration of the combustion products out the back of the engine. This means that to produce a large thrust, you need a lot of propellant that burns fast and shoots its combustion products rapidly out of the engine. If the exhaust is smaller or moves more slowly, thrust will be smaller.

SOLID PROPELLANTS

The first rockets used solid propellants to produce thrust. A solid propellant is dry to the touch. It contains both the fuel and the oxidizer already mixed together. Chinese fire rockets used solid propellants and, in recent years, the space shuttle launched using solid propellant rocket boosters.

Whether on a fire arrow or a space shuttle, the design for a solid-propellant rocket is fairly simple. All solid-fuel rockets work in the same way. The fuel burns and produces hot exhaust gases. These gases escape from the bottom of the rocket, which makes the rocket fly into the air.

WORDS TO KNOW

insulated: covered with a material that limits the transfer of heat.

The rocket has a case or tube that carries the packed propellant. In early rockets, this case was made from materials such as paper, leather, or iron. Modern rockets use propellant cases made from aluminum, which is a thin, lightweight metal. Because aluminum is thin, it could melt when the propellant burns. To prevent melting, the inside of the aluminum case is **insulated** to protect it from the propellant's heat.

CHINESE FIRE ROCKETS

The Chinese packed gunpowder into a cylinder and sealed one end. The gunpowder contained potassium nitrate, a substance that provided the oxygen needed for the other chemicals in the gunpowder to burn rapidly. Once ignited, the gunpowder emitted large amounts of gas and combustion products out the open end of the cylinder that created thrust, and the arrow shot into the air.

The top of the propellant case is sealed, often with the payload or recovery parachutes. The bottom of the case narrows to a small opening called the throat. By narrowing this opening, pressure inside the case builds as the burning releases hot, expanding gases.

Have you ever played with a garden hose? When the sprayer is fully open, the water flows out wide and light. When the sprayer is adjusted and the opening is narrowed, that water stream also narrows and increases in force.

When a solid propellant is packed inside the rocket's insulated case, it can be packed as a solid mass. When ignited, the propellant burns from one end to the other. If the rocket is large, it may take some time to burn all of the propellant inside the case.

Another method packs the propellant inside the insulated case with a **hollow core**. When ignited, the entire **surface area** of the core burns outward from the core to the inside of the case. This method causes the propellant to burn more quickly, because more of the propellant's surface area is burning at the same time. A solid propellant also needs an **igniter** to light the propellant and start it burning.

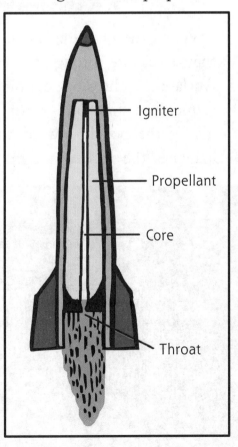

Igniter

Propellant

Core

Throat

ROCKETRY

The Chinese used **fuses** to ignite the gunpowder in their fire arrows. The problem with fuses, however, is that they are unpredictable and dangerous. If a fuse burns too quickly, the person lighting it may not have enough time to move a safe distance away before the rocket launches.

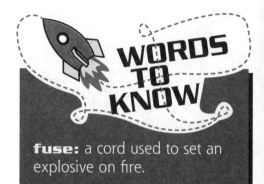

WORDS TO KNOW

fuse: a cord used to set an explosive on fire.

Later, electric ignition systems replaced fuses. A wire heated and ignited the propellant. Other rockets, such as the space shuttle's solid rocket boosters, use small rocket motors deep inside the hollow core.

WHEN THE SMALL ROCKET IS IGNITED, IT SHOOTS FLAMES DOWN THE CORE, WHICH IGNITE THE ENTIRE SURFACE OF THE HOLLOW CORE.

When the building pressure forces the gases out of the opening, they accelerate through the cone-shaped structure called the nozzle. At launch, the nozzle points straight down toward the ground. Remember Newton's third law? When the escaping gases rush out of the nozzle toward the ground, the opposite reaction force launches the rocket straight into the air.

CORE SHAPE

To help the propellant burn faster, some rockets use different core shapes to increase the surface area burned. The space shuttle used star-shaped cores. The additional surface area of the star shape allowed the propellant to burn more quickly, which gave the shuttle's rockets more thrust power during launch. What other core shapes would give the flame more surface area to burn?

LIQUID PROPELLANTS

In the late nineteenth and early twentieth centuries, rocket scientists such as Robert Goddard and Konstantin Tsiolkovsky realized that solid propellants could not give a rocket enough thrust to launch into orbit. Instead, they believed that liquid propellants could be more powerful. Experimenting with liquid-propulsion systems, Goddard launched the first successful flight of a rocket with a liquid fuel in 1926.

A LIQUID-PROPELLANT ROCKET IS MUCH MORE COMPLEX THAN A SOLID-PROPELLANT ROCKET.

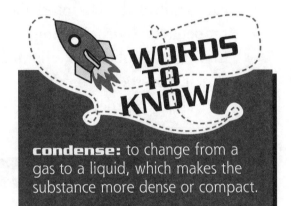

WORDS TO KNOW

condense: to change from a gas to a liquid, which makes the substance more dense or compact.

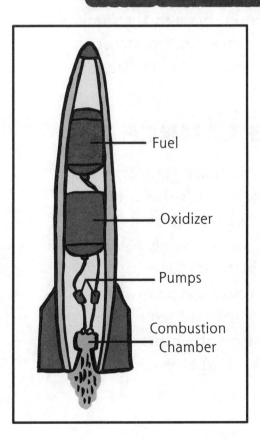

Fuel

Oxidizer

Pumps

Combustion Chamber

Liquid-propulsion systems use a liquid fuel such as kerosene or liquid hydrogen. The oxidizer is usually pure oxygen that has been chilled so that it **condenses** into liquid form. Unlike the solid propellant's fuel and oxidizer, liquid fuel and its oxidizer cannot be stored together because the two substances ignite on contact.

Therefore, a liquid-propellant rocket carries two large tanks. One tank holds the fuel, while the other holds the oxidizer. High-speed pumps shoot the fuel and oxidizer into a combustion chamber. As they mix, they ignite and create large quantities of hot gas combustion products.

Liquid-propellant systems have several advantages over solid propellants. Combinations of liquid fuel and oxidizer that ignite upon contact do not need an ignition system. In addition, engineers can control liquid propellants better than solid propellants. By controlling the flow of fuel and oxidizer into the combustion chamber, engineers control the amount of thrust the rocket produces at any time. Engineers can also stop and start the rocket engine, simply by stopping and restarting the flow of liquid propellants.

DID YOU KNOW?
Many liquid fuels are really cold gases stored under pressure.

THE ADVANTAGES OF LIQUID PROPELLANTS COME WITH A COST.

Liquid-propellant engines are more complex than solid-propellant systems. As a result, they fail more frequently. Because the liquid systems need more equipment, such as tanks and combustion chambers, they are also heavier. The more mass a rocket has, the harder it is to launch.

HOW MASS AFFECTS LAUNCH

Imagine throwing a rock in your back yard. If you're simply tossing a pebble, you don't have to use much arm strength or force to send it flying. On the other hand, if you're trying to throw a large rock, you had better make sure you've been doing push-ups! You're going to have to use your arm muscles to generate more force in order to toss the larger rock the same distance as the smaller pebble. Why is this true?

NEWTONS AND KILOGRAMS

Weight and mass are confusing because people usually talk about weight in terms of pounds and kilograms, which change according to what planet you're on, while mass is also measured in kilograms, which stay the same no matter where in the universe you are! To make things simpler, many scientists measure weight in newtons. Newtons refer to how much gravitational force is exerted on a body's mass. One kilogram of mass is equal to 9.8 newtons. So if the scale says 60 pounds, which is 27 kilograms, you can also say you are 265 newtons! The number of newtons you weigh changes as you move from Earth to the moon to Jupiter, but your 27 kilograms of mass always stays the same.

What exactly is mass? Is it how much something weighs? Mass is not the same as weight. Weight is determined by an object's mass and the force of gravity on the object. So you might weigh 60 pounds (27 kilograms or 265 newtons) on Earth. But on the moon, where there is a much weaker gravitational pull on your body, your weight would be much less, only 10 pounds (4 kilograms or 44 newtons). On Jupiter, which has a strong gravitational pull, you'd weigh about 142 pounds (64 kilograms or 628 newtons)!

In contrast, mass stays the same no matter what planet you're on. Mass is the amount of matter in an object. Your mass is the same on Earth, in space, or on the moon. An object with mass does not have to be solid. Mass can be the amount of air in a balloon or the amount of water in a glass.

EARTH
60 Pounds

MOON
10 Pounds

JUPITER
142 Pounds

ROCKETRY

The total mass of a rocket has a big impact on its performance. The greater a rocket's mass, the more weight it will have, because weight = mass x gravity. The rocket's engine will have to generate enough thrust to overcome the gravitational force pushing downward on the rocket.

IF THE ROCKET'S WEIGHT IS GREATER THAN THE THRUST ITS ENGINES CAN PRODUCE, IT WILL REMAIN ON THE LAUNCH PAD.

One of the heaviest things on a rocket is its propellant. There are no fuel stations in the air or in space. Therefore, a rocket has to carry onboard enough propellant for its entire mission. Because they can't change the propellant's mass, engineers look for other ways to lighten a rocket's load.

MASS FRACTION

Rocket engineers use a calculation called **mass fraction (MF)** to measure the effectiveness of a rocket's design. Mass fraction is calculated by:

MF = mass of the propellant ÷ mass of the total rocket

The larger the MF, the smaller the payload the rocket can carry. In other words, if propellant is a larger portion of the rocket's total mass, the rocket cannot carry much payload. The trade-off, however, is that the smaller the rocket's MF, the lower its range. The most efficient rockets have an MF of approximately 0.91. The ideal rocket has 91 percent of its mass in its propellants and 6 percent in its payload. The other 3 percent is in the rocket's tanks, engines, and fins. This value allows for an effective balance between payload and range.

WORDS TO KNOW

mass fraction (MF): a calculation used to measure the balance between payload and range, which is the effectiveness of a rocket's design.

One way engineers reduce the rocket's weight is by making its structure lighter. They use lightweight materials strengthened by ribs to build engine tanks. They chill hydrogen and oxygen propellants until they become liquid, which reduces their total **volume**. This allows the rocket to use smaller, lighter tanks to carry the liquid propellants. Engineers also design the rocket's nozzle from lightweight metals. The thin metals are insulated to protect them from the intense heat of the burning propellants.

MULTI-STAGING

When building a rocket to be powerful enough to reach outer space, engineers face a dilemma. To reach space, a rocket needs to carry a lot of propellant. To carry that much fuel, it needs to have some big tanks and equipment. But when a rocket gets too big, its mass also becomes very large. A rocket with a large mass will have a very strong gravitational force pulling it to the earth. How will it be able to create enough thrust to overcome gravity?

> **HOW CAN ENGINEERS DESIGN A ROCKET THAT BALANCES POWER AND MASS TO CARRY ASTRONAUTS TO THE MOON?**

The solution to this dilemma is a technique called staging. Remember the sixteenth-century German fireworks maker, Johann Schmidlap, who you read about in Chapter 1? By attaching a small rocket to the top of a larger rocket, Schmidlap's fireworks soared to greater heights than ever before.

Engineers use the staging technique to build rockets that can reach outer space, the moon, and other planets. In **serial staging**, engineers stack several small rockets or stages on top of a larger rocket. Each stage has its own propellant, engines, instruments, and frame. The rocket's payload is usually protected in a nose cone at the top of the stack.

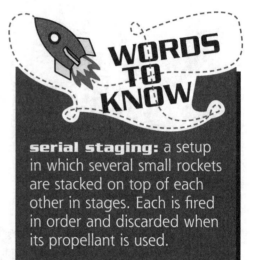

serial staging: a setup in which several small rockets are stacked on top of each other in stages. Each is fired in order and discarded when its propellant is used.

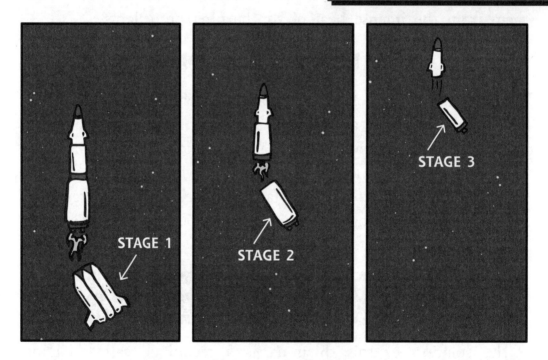

STAGE 1

STAGE 2

STAGE 3

The first stage is powerful enough to lift its own mass, as well as the mass of all the other stages. When the first stage burns through its propellant, it drops off. The second rocket, or second stage, fires. When it burns through its propellant, it also drops off and the third stage fires.

WHEN ONE OF THE ROCKET'S STAGES DROPS OFF, THE ROCKET'S TOTAL MASS IS LESS.

When a stage drops off, it leaves less mass for the remaining stages to propel. This allows the second and third stages to operate more efficiently because the rocket's total mass is lower. With each remaining stage, it is easier to create thrust to accelerate the rocket with less propellant. The Saturn V moon rockets used three-stage serial staging.

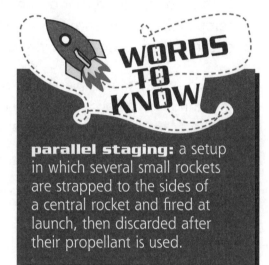

parallel staging: a setup in which several small rockets are strapped to the sides of a central rocket and fired at launch, then discarded after their propellant is used.

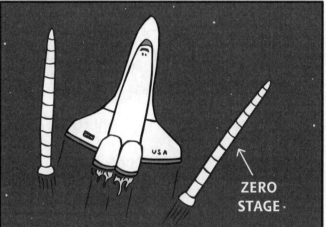

ZERO STAGE

Another type of staging is called **parallel staging**. Several small rockets are strapped to the sides of a central rocket. These small outer rockets are called zero stages. All of the rockets are ignited at launch.

When the smaller rockets have burned all of their propellant, they drop off. The central rocket continues burning and carries the payload to its destination. The space shuttle used parallel staging.

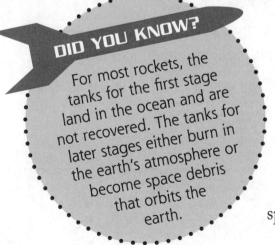

DID YOU KNOW?

For most rockets, the tanks for the first stage land in the ocean and are not recovered. The tanks for later stages either burn in the earth's atmosphere or become space debris that orbits the earth.

$v = \sqrt{G\dfrac{M}{r}}$

TWO-STAGE ROCKET BALLOON

To generate enough thrust to enable a rocket to travel longer distances, scientists design multi-stage rockets. In this project, create your own multi-stage rocket and compare its performance to a single-stage rocket. Start a scientific method worksheet in your science journal.

SUPPLIES

- ☊ science journal and pencil
- ☊ scissors
- ☊ straw
- ☊ 20 feet (6 meters) of string
- ☊ 2 points to attach the string—chairs, trees, fence posts
- ☊ small paper cup
- ☊ 2 oblong balloons
- ☊ tape

1 Cut the straw into four pieces and thread each piece onto the string. Tie the ends of the string to the two attach points. Make sure your string is taut.

2 Cut out the bottom of the paper cup. Slide the rim of the cup over balloon #1 and pull the balloon's neck through the cup's bottom. Inflate the balloon and pinch the neck closed.

BALLOON #2   **BALLOON #1**

3 Have a helper insert balloon #2 in the open bottom of the cup and inflate it. The cup should be snug enough around the inflated balloon #2 to hold #1's neck closed and in place. Pinch the neck of balloon #2 shut.

4 While your assistant holds the rocket and pinches #2 closed, tape the rocket to the four straw pieces. Attach balloon #1 to two pieces of straw. Attach balloon #2 to the remaining two pieces of straw on either side of the cup.

5 Release the neck of balloon #2. What happens? How does this compare to the single-stage balloon rocket in Chapter 2? Which balloon rocket goes farthest?

Try This: Adjust the size of the balloons and repeat the experiment. Which design allows the rocket to travel the farthest distance? Which design allows the rocket to travel the fastest?

$\dfrac{v^2}{r} = g$

$$\frac{v^2}{r} = g$$

FILM-CANISTER ROCKET

When two substances are mixed together, they can cause a chemical reaction. Traditional rockets use chemical reactions to produce thrust for launch. In this project, you will see how two common substances, baking soda and vinegar, can launch a rocket in your back yard. Start a scientific method worksheet in your science journal. **Caution: You must wear safety glasses during this experiment.**

1 Put on your safety glasses before you begin this experiment. Go outside to launch your rocket.

2 To insert the chemical fuel, remove the film canister's cover. Put a small amount of baking soda in the canister. Add some vinegar and quickly replace the cover.

3 Quickly place the canister upside down on the ground or other surface. Stand back for launch!

What's Happening? Combining baking soda and vinegar generates carbon dioxide gas. The gas is trapped in the film canister, where the pressure builds up. What happens when the pressure from the gas becomes greater than the pressure from the canister lid?

Try This: Vary the proportions of baking soda and vinegar in your rocket. Record your observations. What combination creates the most force? How can you tell?

$$v = \sqrt{G\frac{M}{r}}$$

ROCKET CAR

You can use a chemical reaction between water and an antacid tablet to power a rocket car and demonstrate Newton's laws of motion. Alka-Seltzer contains a substance called bicarbonate. When bicarbonate mixes with water, carbon dioxide gas is produced. What happens when carbon dioxide gas is produced in a film canister? What do you think will happen if you attach the canister to a toy car? **Caution: You must wear safety glasses during this experiment.**

SUPPLIES

- safety glasses
- outdoor area such as driveway or sidewalk
- empty film canister
- tape
- toy car, about 2 inches (5 centimeters) long
- water
- Alka-Seltzer tablet broken into 4 pieces

1 Before you begin, put on safety glasses. You may want to have an adult help you with this activity.

2 Tape the canister to the back of the toy car. Point the open end of the canister toward the rear of the car.

3 Holding the car upright, fill the canister about halfway with clean water. Add one piece of the Alka-Seltzer tablet, then quickly put the lid on the canister and set the car on the ground. Move several feet away.

What's Happening? Can you explain the action using Newton's third law of motion?

Try This: Change the amount of Alka-Seltzer you put in the canister. How does this change the car's speed and distance traveled?

$$\frac{v^2}{r} = g$$

ROCKET-POWERED SKATEBOARD

SUPPLIES

- science journal and pencil
- safety glasses
- duct tape
- Mentos candy, white mint
- rubber cork
- 2-liter bottle of diet soda
- skateboard

Soda is bubbly because of carbon dioxide gas that has been forced into the liquid. When you shake a soda and then open the can, the gas is quickly released. When you add Mentos candies into a soda, the chemical reaction between the two creates a lot of foam. How can you use this science to make a super-speedy skateboard? Start a scientific method worksheet in your science journal.

1 **Put on safety glasses.** Tape together a stack of five Mentos and tape this stack to the bottom of the cork.

2 Tape the soda bottle to the skateboard so the neck sticks out the back of the skateboard like a car's exhaust pipe.

CORK

DUCT TAPE

MENTOS

3 Pour out enough soda so that the top 2 inches (5 centimeters) of the bottle are air. Keeping the bottle upright, insert the Mentos stack and rubber cork into the neck and press firmly. You do not want the candies to be touching the soda at this point—pour out more soda if needed. Put the skateboard on the ground and quickly step a few feet away.

What's Happening? What did you use to create a force strong enough to move the skateboard? Is the skateboard moving in the same direction as the soda or in the opposite direction? Why? What law explains this?

Try This: Repeat your experiment with different sodas. Vary the number of Mentos. Make a chart to show how these changes affect your skateboard rocket. What combination creates the best launch?

$$v = \sqrt{G\frac{M}{r}}$$

WATER-BOTTLE ROCKET

Newton's third law states that for every action, there is an equal and opposite reaction. You can use water pressure, which is the force created when water is **compressed**, to generate thrust and launch a water rocket into the air. Start a scientific method worksheet in your science journal. **Caution: This activity can be messy, so make sure you do it outside with an adult to help. You must wear safety glasses during this experiment.**

1 Put on your safety glasses and go outside.

2 Insert the inflating needle into the cork the long way until its opening comes through the other end. Attach the needle to the bicycle pump.

3 Fill the soda bottle about 75 percent with water.

4 Put the cork into the bottle, making sure that it fits snugly but is not too tight.

5 Put the bottle on the ground, on its side. Point the cork end of the bottle toward an open outdoor space. Make sure it is not pointing toward you or any other people.

WORDS TO KNOW

compress: to squeeze and squish something to make it smaller.

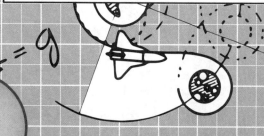

6 Pump air into the bottle with the bicycle pump. You should see air bubbles in the water if the pump is working correctly.

7 Keep pumping until the pressure in the bottle causes the cork to pop out.

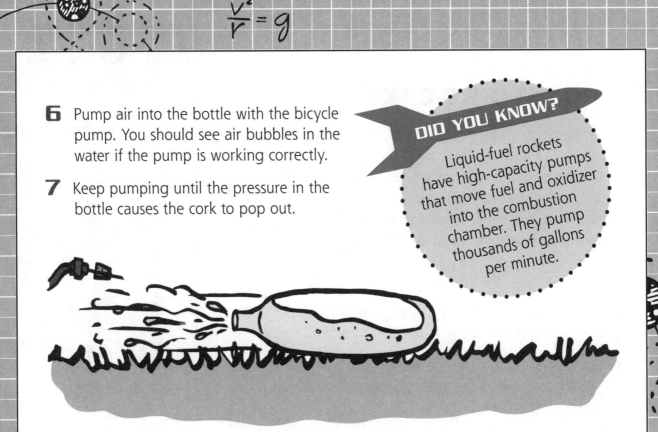

DID YOU KNOW?

Liquid-fuel rockets have high-capacity pumps that move fuel and oxidizer into the combustion chamber. They pump thousands of gallons per minute.

What's Happening? What happens to your water rocket? Which direction is the air going? How about the water?

Try This: Repeat this activity using different amounts of water in the bottle. Increasing the amount of water will increase the mass of your water-bottle rocket. What water level gives you the best launch? How did the rocket's mass affect your launch? Use a chart to record your observations in your scientific method worksheet.

	75 PERCENT	50 PERCENT	25 PERCENT
Distance Traveled			
Time			

$$\frac{v^2}{r} = g$$

$$v = \sqrt{G\frac{M}{r}}$$

POTATO ROCKET

In this activity, you will use air pressure to launch a potato. Because the potato can travel long distances, this activity should be performed outside, in a wide-open space. Start a scientific method worksheet in your science journal. **Caution: You must wear safety glasses during this experiment. Have an adult nearby to assist.**

1 Put on your safety glasses.

2 Put a potato on the ground and push one end of the pipe into the potato to lodge a piece of it inside the pipe.

3 Have an adult help you use the broomstick to push the potato deeper into the pipe. Stop when the potato is about one-third of the way down. Remove the broomstick.

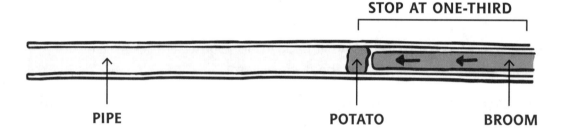

STOP AT ONE-THIRD

PIPE   POTATO   BROOM

4 Put another potato on the ground and push the other end of the pipe (the end that's farther away from your potato inside) into the potato to stick it on the end of the pipe.

SUPPLIES

- ☊ science journal and pencil
- ☊ safety glasses
- ☊ potatoes
- ☊ PVC pipe, 4 feet (about 1 meter) long by 1 inch (2½ centimeters) in diameter
- ☊ broomstick, with a diameter narrower than the pipe

$v = \sqrt{G\frac{M}{r}}$

$\frac{v^2}{r} = g$

$$\frac{v^2}{r} = g$$

POP

5 Prepare to launch. Make sure the potato
end of your pipe is not pointing toward any
people or objects. Quickly force the broomstick into the
pipe. What's the best way to do this?

What's Happening? What happens to the potato on the end of the
pipe? Why?

Try This: Repeat this activity launching your potato at different angles. Use
the pictures and chart below to record your observations in your science journal.
What happens when you launch at a 20-degree angle? A 45-degree angle? A
90-degree angle? Make sure you watch where the potato goes so it doesn't land
on you! Which angle makes the potato travel the farthest distance? Why do you
think this happens?

	20 DEGREES	**45 DEGREES**	**90 DEGREES**
	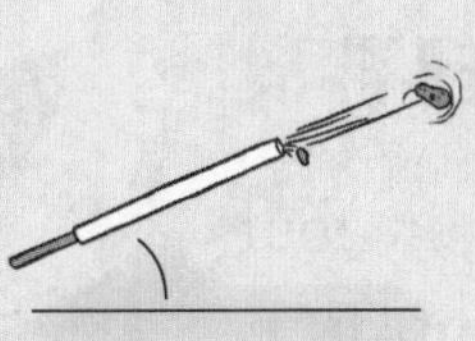	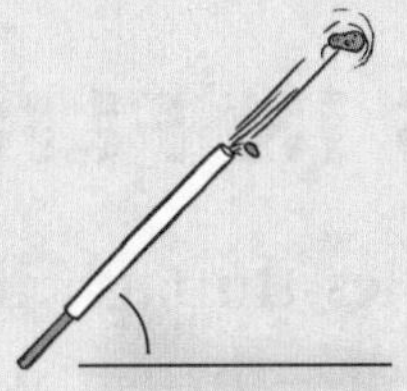	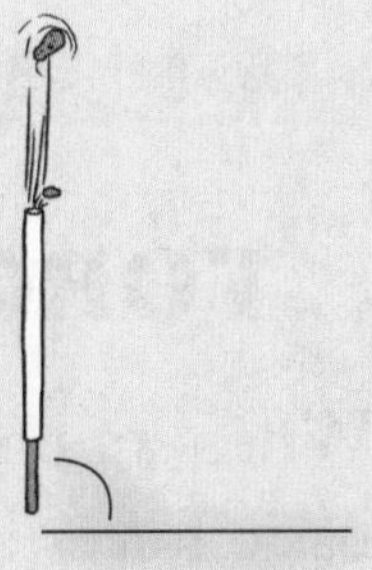
Distance Traveled			

$$v = \sqrt{G\frac{M}{r}}$$

— CHAPTER 5 —
ROCKETS IN FLIGHT

Now you know how a rocket launches off the ground.
But what happens after that? How do we control
where it goes, how far it travels, and how fast it flies?
Let's go back to physics to find the answers.

FORCES IN FLIGHT

When an object flies through the air, four basic forces act on it—thrust, weight, **lift**, and drag. These forces push an object up or down. They propel it forward or slow it down. Together, these forces play a big part in how a rocket flies.

WORDS TO KNOW

lift: an aerodynamic force that pushes upward on an object in flight.

You've learned that thrust moves an object forward. Jet airplanes create thrust by pulling air through an engine, while rockets create thrust with a propellant system. While thrust pushes an object forward, drag works in the opposite direction. Drag will cause an object to slow down as it moves through air.

What happens when you try to walk forward into a strong wind? Can you feel a drag force pushing against you, slowing down your movement? Drag is caused by friction between air and an object's surface. Larger objects that have more surface area experience more drag.

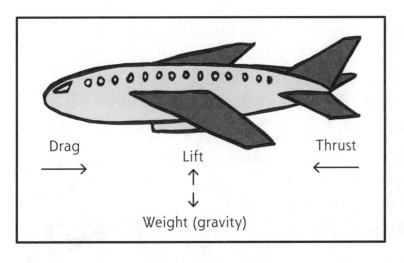

Drag →   Lift ↑ ↓   Thrust ←   Weight (gravity)

WEIGHT IS CAUSED BY THE FORCE OF GRAVITY PULLING ON AN OBJECT.

A rocket's weight depends on its mass, which is the amount of matter in an object. An object with more mass has more weight. In the atmosphere, lift is a force that holds an object in the air, opposing the force of weight. Lift pushes upward underneath an object.

If the air pressure is stronger on the underside of an object, lift pushes it upward. The wings of airplanes are designed to make use of lift, but on a rocket, lift is generally not a significant force.

When the four forces of thrust, weight, lift, and drag are equal and balanced, an object flies a level path. If lift and thrust are stronger than the forces of gravity and drag, the object flies higher. On the other hand, if gravity and drag are stronger than lift and thrust, the object moves down toward the earth. This follows Newton's second law—a change in an object's motion is equal to the size of an external force acting on it and the exact direction of the force.

All Forces
are Equal

Stronger Lift
and Thrust

Stronger Drag and
Weight (gravity)

To understand the four forces in flight, imagine throwing a baseball in your back yard. When you throw the ball, your arm gives it thrust to send it moving forward through the air. As it moves, the ball's spin creates lift that pushes on the bottom of the ball, keeping it in the air.

At the same time, drag from the air pushes against the ball, in the opposite direction of its movement. This slows the ball down. The ball's weight also pulls it toward the ground. Eventually, weight and drag overcome thrust and lift, causing the ball to curve downward and land on the ground.

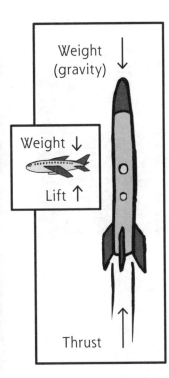

Weight (gravity) ↓

Weight ↓ Lift ↑

Thrust

Although these four forces affect all objects in flight, there are some differences in how the forces affect rockets. On a rocket during launch, thrust works opposite weight, propelling the rocket upward against gravity's pull toward Earth. On airplanes, lift works opposite weight, pushing the plane up while its weight pulls it down.

With an airplane, drag and lift are created by the plane's wings and tail. Because a rocket does not have wings, drag and lift are created by its fins, nose cone, and body. In rockets, drag is typically much stronger than lift.

During an airplane's flight, the four forces generally remain the same. During a rocket's flight, the size and direction of the forces acting on the rocket can change significantly.

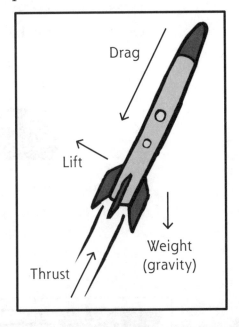

Drag

Lift

Weight (gravity)

Thrust

FORCE CONTROL

Armies of Mysore, a region of what is now India, used rockets in battle against the British in the 1700s. These early rockets were **unstable** and difficult to control. They flew **erratically**, **tumbled** in the air, and changed directions. The Mysore used this to their advantage, and attached blades to the rockets that would spin around and cut anything in their paths. Why is it important for scientists to understand how forces affect a rocket's motion?

Understanding how forces affect a rocket's motion helped scientists design rocket control systems to stabilize and steer rockets.

WORDS TO KNOW

unstable: not steady, unpredictable.

erratic: moving in an irregular pattern.

tumble: to fall helplessly, turning over and over.

CENTER OF MASS

All matter has a point called the **center of mass (CM)**, or center of gravity. The CM is the average location of the object's mass. This is the point where the object can be perfectly balanced. To illustrate this idea, try balancing a pen on your finger. What happens?

WORDS TO KNOW

center of mass (CM): the point on an object where its mass is equally balanced on both sides.

> AT ONE POINT, THE PEN WILL BALANCE PERFECTLY. THIS POINT IS THE PEN'S CM.

Its mass on one side of your finger is balanced with the mass on the other side of your finger. If you were to add something to one end of the pen, such as an eraser or sticky chewing gum, the pen would no longer balance at that same point. The pen's CM would be closer to the end with the gum.

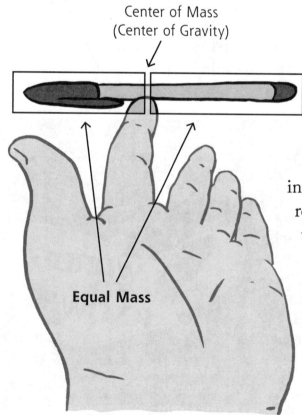

Center of Mass (Center of Gravity)

Equal Mass

A rocket's CM affects its stability in flight. When a rocket flies, it rotates around its CM. If it is unstable, it will begin to tumble in the air instead of rotating around the CM. When the rocket tumbles, more surface area hits the flowing air. This increases the drag acting on the rocket, and the rocket slows down.

CENTER OF PRESSURE

A rocket also has a point called the **center of pressure (CP)** that affects its flight. When a rocket is in flight, air flows past it, creating drag and lift. The air pushes and rubs against the rocket's surfaces. This can cause the rocket to move and turn. The center of pressure is the average location of the drag and lift forces on the rocket.

WORDS TO KNOW

center of pressure (CP): the point on an object in the air where the drag and lift forces acting on it are equal.

THE CENTER OF PRESSURE ONLY EXISTS WHEN THE ROCKET IS FLYING IN THE AIR.

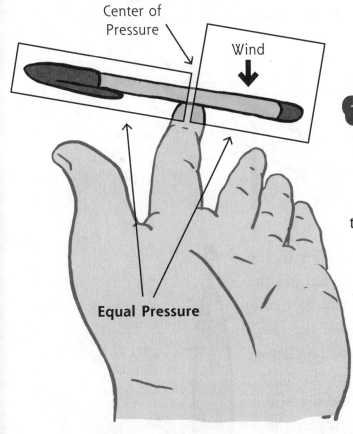

Center of Pressure

Wind

Equal Pressure

To think about CP, imagine trying to balance a pen on your hand while the wind is blowing on one side of the pen. The spot where you can balance the pen moves. The CP depends on positions of the pen's parts and on how hard the wind presses on each part.

What if you added a fin to the end of the pen? How would that new shape affect the pen's CP?

ROCKETRY

A weathervane looks like an arrow mounted on top of a pole. It has a small arrowhead at one end and a larger tail at the other end. The arrow balances on a vertical pole at its CM. People use weathervanes to tell which direction the wind is blowing.

When the wind blows, the air pushes with greater force on the vane's tail, because it has a larger surface area to hit. The flowing air pushes the tail away. If it pushes it too far, the flowing air on the other side will push the tail back. At the vane's CP, the air flows with equal pressure on both sides and the vane points directly into the wind.

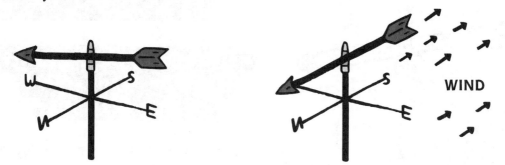

For a rocket to be stable when it flies in the atmosphere, its CP should be located behind the CM and closer to its tail. One way to make the rocket more stable is to increase the size of its fins or place them closer to the rocket's tail, which moves the CP closer to the tail. Another way to make a rocket more stable is to make its nose heavier. This moves the CM closer to the rocket's nose and increases the distance between the CM and the CP.

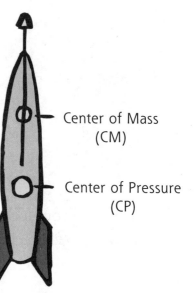

Center of Mass (CM)

Center of Pressure (CP)

CONTROL SYSTEMS: PASSIVE

To improve rocket performance, scientists design control systems for stability. The simplest control system is a **passive control system**. Passive controls are fixed devices. They stabilize the rocket simply by being attached to the rocket's body. When a rocket begins to move away from its original path, passive controls act to bring it back to its original path.

WORDS TO KNOW

passive control system: fixed controls that stabilize a rocket.

A Chinese fire arrow uses a very simple passive control: a stick attached to the end of the rocket. The stick caused the fire arrow's CP to fall behind its CM.

Fins mounted on a rocket's body are another type of passive control system. Fins have a large surface area, which keeps the CP behind the rocket's CM. If a rocket begins to fishtail or move from side to side, the fins create drag in the flowing air. They direct the airflow to one side, which causes the rocket to move in the opposite way and corrects the unstable fishtailing. This follows Newton's third law—every action has an equal and opposite reaction.

FINS

Fins are a passive control. When fins are placed near the back of a rocket, behind its center of mass, they provide stability. The fins work by providing drag that keeps the back of the rocket from tumbling in front of the rocket's nose. To work effectively, fins need to be placed near the rear of the rocket. Engineers also try to design fins that are as small as possible to minimize drag, while also keeping them large enough to stabilize the rocket's flight. Since fins increase a rocket's weight and reduce its range, today they are only used as a control system for model rockets and small missiles.

CONTROL SYSTEMS: ACTIVE

Active control systems can be moved in flight to stabilize the rocket as conditions change. Active controls also allow the rocket to change its course during flight. Vanes, **movable fins, canards**, gimbaled nozzles, and **vernier rockets** are examples of active control systems.

During flight, movable fins and canards can tilt like the rudder on a boat. Fins are located near the tail of the rocket, while canards are closer to the front of the rocket. Their movement deflects the airflow around the rocket, which causes the rocket to change its course.

active control system: controls that can be moved during flight to stabilize and steer a rocket.

movable fins: fins attached to a rocket that can be tilted to stabilize a rocket.

canards: small movable fins attached near the nose of a rocket that can be tilted during flight.

vernier rocket: a very small rocket used to make exact adjustments to the flight of a large rocket.

MOVABLE FINS AND CANARDS ARE SMALLER AND LIGHTER THAN LARGER, PASSIVE FINS AND PRODUCE LESS DRAG.

Vanes are like small fins placed inside the rocket's exhaust pipe. When the vanes tilt, they change the direction of the exhaust gas and the rocket points the opposite way. A gimbaled nozzle also changes the direction of the exhaust. When the nozzle tilts in one direction, the rocket's nose moves in the opposite direction, changing the rocket's course.

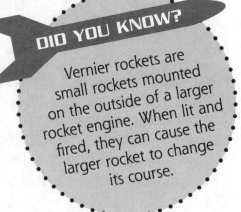

DID YOU KNOW?

Vernier rockets are small rockets mounted on the outside of a larger rocket engine. When lit and fired, they can cause the larger rocket to change its course.

ROCKETS IN FLIGHT

Once a rocket leaves the atmosphere, there is no air for active controls to use. Instead of using movable fins and canards, rockets use attitude-control rockets to control movement in space. These are small engine clusters that are fixed all over a space vehicle. When attitude-control rockets are fired in certain combinations, the space vehicle changes direction.

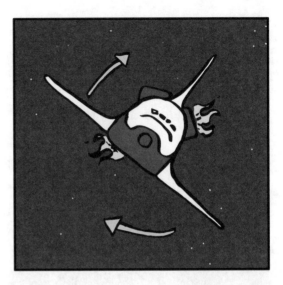

ROCKET BELT

The Rocket Belt was the first personal rocket pack. It was built in the 1960s by Bell Aerosystems for the U.S. Army. The Belt was a 120-pound backpack with controls, fuel tanks, and two nozzles. The belt used hydrogen peroxide as fuel, which was broken down into a mixture of steam and oxygen that blasted out of two nozzles and propelled the pack and its wearer.

The pilot could change the direction of the pack's thrust by using hand-operated controls to move the direction of the nozzles. Leaning forward or backward to move, the wearer flew in an upright position. The belt could only carry enough fuel to fly for about 20 seconds. Although the Army no longer uses the Rocket Belt, amateur rocket hobbyists are still flying with rocket packs and improving the design.

PS Watch video footage of Rocket Belt tests. Can you think of some uses for these had they been safe?

CONTROLLING THRUST

Controlling thrust is an important part of directing a rocket's flight. If a rocket's thrust is either too short or too long, it will send its payload into the wrong orbit. If placed in the wrong spot, a satellite may be useless. It may be too far into space to send back a signal. Or it could be too close to the atmosphere and fall back to Earth.

DID YOU KNOW?

The firing of small rockets to put a spacecraft into the right orbit is called a burn. For spacecraft traveling to Mars or other planets, the craft has a large burn shortly after leaving Earth's atmosphere. The burn puts the spacecraft onto the correct path.

For rockets that use a liquid-propellant system, a computer controls thrust. It starts the flow of propellants into the combustion chamber. The computer can stop the engine by stopping the flow of propellants. On a long mission, the computer might start and stop the rocket's engine several times.

CONTROLLING THRUST IS NOT AS EASY IN ROCKETS THAT USE SOLID PROPELLANTS.

Once a solid propellant begins to burn, it is very difficult to stop. Some solid-fuel rockets use fire extinguishers and hatches to slow or stop burning in an emergency. Most of the time, however, engineers plan the rocket's **burn rate** very carefully, so that they will not need to stop and restart the engine.

WORDS TO KNOW

burn rate: a measure of how fast a solid propellant burns.

$$\frac{v^2}{r} = g$$

FOAM ROCKETS

To use your air-powered rocket launcher from page 44, create a supply of foam rockets to launch. You can use these foam rockets for several of the projects in this book.

1. Using scissors, cut a piece of foam pipe insulation about 12 inches (30 centimeters) long. This will be the body of your rocket.

2. Use duct tape to close off the top of the foam piece so the blast of air from the launcher will create air pressure to propel the rocket upward. This is the nose of your rocket.

3. Cut four small slits at the base of the rocket body, spacing them evenly around.

4. To make the fins, notch a pair of index cards by cutting halfway down the center on the long side of both cards. Push the index cards together, notches facing, to form an "X". Secure the assembly with tape.

5. Slide the assembled fins into the slits on the foam rocket and glue them in place.

6. Repeat steps 1 through 5 to make several rockets. Allow the glue to dry completely before using the rockets.

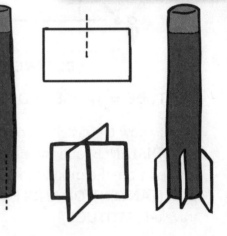

7. To test one of your foam rockets on the rocket launcher, attach an empty 2-liter soda bottle to the end of the launcher by screwing it into the glued-on cap.

8. **Put on your safety glasses.** Place a foam rocket on the piece of PVC that's sticking up. **Make sure the rocket isn't pointing toward anyone or anything.** Stomp on the bottle and blast off!

$$v = \sqrt{G\frac{M}{r}}$$

ESTIMATE ALTITUDE

How do you know how high your rocket flies? A simple technique called triangulation can help you estimate its altitude. Triangulation is based on a branch of mathematics called trigonometry. Trigonometry allows you to figure out the length of a triangle's third side if you know that side's angle and the lengths of the other two sides. You will be using the formula and diagram below to estimate your rocket's altitude.

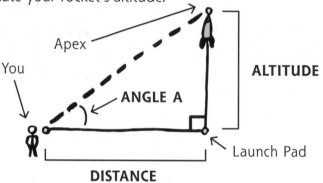

Apex

You

ALTITUDE

ANGLE A

Launch Pad

DISTANCE

ALTITUDE = TANGENT OF ANGLE A x DISTANCE

If you know the distance you are from the rocket launch pad (**DISTANCE**) and the **tangent of the angle** formed from the ground to the **apex** of your rocket's path (**TANGENT OF ANGLE A**), you can figure out the vertical distance your rocket traveled (**ALTITUDE**)!

1 To determine the tangent of Angle A, you'll first need to make a viewing tool. Use a protractor to mark angle lines in 15-degree increments on a piece of cardboard from 0 degrees to 90 degrees, like the diagram shown on the next page.

shown on the next page.

WORDS TO KNOW

tangent of the angle: the length of the opposite side of the triangle divided by the length of the **adjacent** side of the triangle.

adjacent: next to.

apex: the highest point of something.

SUPPLIES

- protractor
- cardboard, approximately 8 by 10 inches (20 by 25 centimeters)
- pen
- 12-inch string
- fishing weight or metal washer
- tape
- empty paper towel tube
- tape measure
- foam rockets and air-powered launcher
- several 2-liter soda bottles
- safety glasses
- scientific calculator

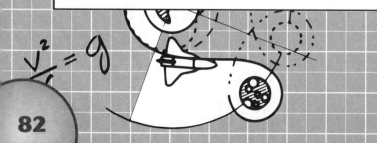

$$\frac{v^2}{r} = g$$

2 Tape one end of the string to the square corner of the cardboard and tie the fishing weight to the other end. Then tape the cardboard tube along the 90-degree line of the cardboard.

ATTACH STRING HERE

90 75 60 45 30 15 0

3 Set your sighting point. This is where you will stand with your sighting tool when you launch the rocket. Measure the distance between the rocket launch pad and the sighting point. This is your **DISTANCE**. For example, let's say your sighting point is 25 feet (7.62 meters) from your launch pad. Your formula would now look like this:
ALTITUDE = TANGENT OF ANGLE A x 25 FEET

ANGLE A

4 **Both you and your friend need to wear safety glasses.** Have a friend launch the rocket while you track it through the sighting tool. Record the angle measured by the tool when the rocket reaches its apex. This is your **ANGLE A**. For our example, let's say you record 30 degrees.

5 Push the "TAN" button on your scientific calculator, enter your **ANGLE A** number, and press "=". This is your **TANGENT OF ANGLE A**. The tangent of 30 degrees is 0.58. Your formula now looks like this: **ALTITUDE = 0.58 x 25 FEET**

6 Now your formula is complete. Use your calculator to figure out your rocket's altitude from your eye-level viewing point.

ALTITUDE = TANGENT OF ANGLE A x DISTANCE

Try This: Your formula uses numbers calculated from your eye-level viewing point. What measurement do you need to add to your altitude to figure out the true altitude of the launch from the ground?

$$v = \sqrt{G\frac{M}{r}}$$

ROCKET MASS

A rocket's mass is an important factor in a rocket's performance. In this experiment, you will test how changing mass can affect a rocket's flight and stability. Start a scientific method worksheet in your science journal.

1 Put on your safety glasses. First launch the rocket without any weights. Use your sighting tool and altitude formula from the previous activity to determine how high your rocket travels. Record your observations about its altitude and performance in a chart like the one below.

2 Increase the rocket's mass by taping metal washers or weights to the rocket body. Repeat the launch and use your chart to record your observations. Continue to add weight to the rocket and launch several times.

What's Happening? How did the different weights affect the rocket's performance and stability? What does this tell you about mass, thrust, and stability?

SUPPLIES

- ∩ science journal and pencil
- ∩ safety glasses
- ∩ foam rocket
- ∩ air-powered launcher
- ∩ several 2-liter soda bottles
- ∩ sighting tool from previous activity
- ∩ measuring tape
- ∩ scientific calculator
- ∩ metal washers or weights
- ∩ tape

NUMBER OF WEIGHTS	ALTITUDE	STABILITY DURING FLIGHT

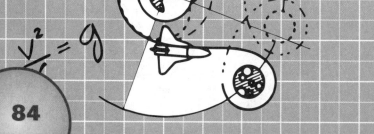

$$\frac{v^2}{r} = g$$

- science journal and pencil
- safety glasses
- foam rockets
- air-powered launcher
- several 2-liter soda bottles
- metal washers or weights
- duct tape

CENTER OF MASS

Where a rocket carries its weight can affect its center of mass, which affects its performance. In this experiment, you will vary a rocket's center of mass to determine how it changes its performance and stability in flight. Start a scientific method worksheet in your science journal.

1 **Put on your safety glasses.**

2 Tape metal washers or weights to the rocket body. Try to find the rocket's center of mass by balancing it on your hand. Record where you placed the weights and where the center of mass is located on the rocket's body.

3 Launch the rocket and record your observations about its performance. How fast does it travel? How far?

4 Using the same amount of weight, change the rocket's center of mass by moving metal washers or weights to another point on the rocket body. Find the new center of mass. Repeat the launch and record your observations.

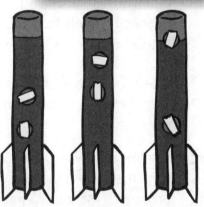

5 Repeat step 4 several times, each time changing the position of the weights and the rocket's center of mass. Record your observations.

6 How did the center of mass affect the rocket's performance and stability? What position of the weight produced the longest distance? Which produced the most stable flight path?

Try This: Build a second rocket that is a different size and mass than your first rocket. Place the weights in the same place on each rocket. Launch the rockets and record your observations. Do the rockets have similar heights and trajectories or are they different?

$$v = \sqrt{G\frac{M}{r}}$$

ROCKET TRAJECTORY

When a rubber band is stretched and released, it snaps back to its original form and releases energy. When used with a foam rocket, this energy can produce enough thrust to launch the rocket. Remember Newton's third law of motion? The rubber band snapping back creates an action force, propelling the rocket forward. At the same time, an opposite and equal force is exerted on the launcher.

When the rocket is launched at an angle of less than 90 degrees, its path is an **arc**. In this experiment, you will test how the launch angle affects the rocket's arc and the distance it travels from the launch pad. Start a scientific method worksheet in your science journal.

SUPPLIES

- ⋒ foam rocket
- ⋒ rubber band
- ⋒ duct tape
- ⋒ protractor
- ⋒ cardboard
- ⋒ scissors
- ⋒ yard stick
- ⋒ tape
- ⋒ push pin
- ⋒ string
- ⋒ metal washer
- ⋒ safety glasses
- ⋒ tape measure

1 Put a rubber band at the rocket's nose and tape it in place. Wrap a second piece of tape to reinforce it.

2 To make a launcher, trace a protractor on a piece of cardboard. Mark the angles at 15-degree intervals. Cut out the pattern.

3 Tape the angle pattern upside down on a yardstick so that the 90-degree line is parallel with the yardstick.

4 Put a push pin through the angle pattern at the point where the 0-degree and 90-degree lines intersect. Tie one end of your string to the pin and the other end to a small weight or washer.

Push Pin

String

Weight

$$\frac{v^2}{r} = g$$

5 **Put on your safety glasses.** To launch a rocket, loop the rubber band over the end of the yardstick. Pull on the rear of the rocket until the rubber band is stretched taut. Note where the nose cone is on the yard stick. Tilt the launcher and read the angle noted by the string. Release the rocket to launch and observe the arc it takes. Measure the distance the rocket traveled from the launch pad. Record your observations.

6 Repeat the launch using a different angle. Make sure you pull the rocket back to the same point on the yardstick each time before releasing it. How does changing the angle affect the flight path and distance traveled by the rocket? What angle allows the rocket to travel the greatest distance?

Try This: Now launch the rocket when its nose cone is aligned at a different point on the yardstick. How does that affect the rocket's performance?

WORDS TO KNOW

arc: a curved path.
ballistic trajectory: the trajectory of an object acted upon by only gravity and drag.

DID YOU KNOW?

When a rocket travels, it might not have enough speed to escape Earth's gravity. It travels a path called a **ballistic trajectory**, curving in an arc until it returns to Earth.

$$v = \sqrt{G\frac{M}{r}}$$

TESTING FIN CONTROL

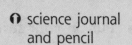

SUPPLIES

- science journal and pencil
- safety glasses
- foam rockets without fins
- air-powered launcher
- several 2-liter soda bottles
- sighting tool from previous activity
- measuring tape
- scientific calculator
- index cards
- scissors
- tape

A rocket without a control system tends to tumble in flight. As it flies, any airflow disturbance exerts a force on the rocket. This force can cause the rocket to move away from its flight path. Without a control system to stabilize it, the rocket will continue to turn and start to tumble. When the rocket tumbles, it has more surface area hitting the flowing air. This increases drag, causing it to slow and fall. You can see how a control system is very important! Start a scientific method worksheet in your science journal.

1 **Put on your safety glasses.** Launch the rocket without any fins. Record your observations in a chart like the one below. How far does it fly? Does it tumble in the air? Does it follow a straight flight path or does it fly off course?

2 Cut out fins from index cards and attach them to the foam rocket.

3 Launch the rocket with fins and record your observations. How does it fly compared to a rocket without fins?

Try This: Experiment with different types of fins. Change the fin size and placement. What fin design produces the most stable rocket performance? Why do you think this occurs?

FIN TYPE	ALTITUDE	STABILITY DURING FLIGHT

— CHAPTER 6 —
COMING BACK TO EARTH: ROCKET RECOVERY SYSTEMS

Everything that goes up, must come down! When early rockets were launched for warfare or fireworks, it did not matter if the rocket returned to Earth safely. These rockets were expected to be used once and destroyed. As rockets began to be used for scientific study, they became more expensive and complex. Payloads carried valuable equipment, data, and astronauts. Engineers tackled a new goal: how to return a rocket safely to Earth.

A rocket recovery system contains the parts of a rocket that are used to help a rocket land without damage. Recovery systems can be very simple or extremely complex. It all depends on the type of rocket.

DRAG RECOVERY SYSTEMS

Simple rocket recovery systems use drag to land safely. Since increasing drag slows the rocket, the rocket has a better chance of landing safely and not suffering damage. As we learned in Chapter 5, drag is a force that opposes an object's motion through air or fluid. Drag is caused by friction between the air or fluid and the surface of the object. Remember trying to walk through a strong wind? It's a lot harder than walking on a windless day. That's because the drag of wind is pushing against you, in the opposite direction of your motion.

> **AN OBJECT'S SHAPE AFFECTS THE DRAG ON IT.**

MODEL ROCKETRY

Model rocketry is an exciting hobby shared by tens of thousands of rocket enthusiasts around the world. Rocketeers build and launch model rockets, from the most simple to very complex. The rocket body is often constructed from a cardboard tube, with a mount for the engine, fins, a parachute, and a nose cone. Some rocketeers attach a tiny camera as the rocket's payload. The camera can be programmed to snap a picture when the rocket reaches its highest point.

A typical model rocket has a motor made from a heavy paper cylinder. The motor has a clay nozzle, propellant, and an ejection charge that will launch a recovery parachute. In the early days of model rocketry, some people were injured from the dangerous chemicals and homemade explosives used to launch model rockets. Today, model rocket motors are made **commercially** and have been tested for safety by the National Association of Rocketry (NAR). The motors come in different sizes so that rocket makers can pick the motors that work best with their rockets.

WORDS TO KNOW

commercially: made by a business.

Objects with a larger surface area experience more drag because there is more of the object for the air to rub against. Think about being in a pool or the ocean. It's a lot easier to swim through water than it is to walk upright through it. When you swim, you're in a horizontal position and **streamlined** to cut through the water.

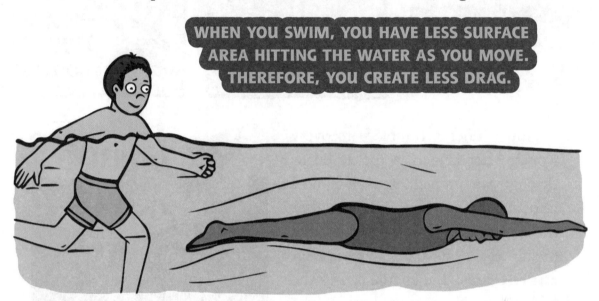

WHEN YOU SWIM, YOU HAVE LESS SURFACE AREA HITTING THE WATER AS YOU MOVE. THEREFORE, YOU CREATE LESS DRAG.

WORDS TO KNOW

streamline: with smooth lines to reduce resistance.

tumble recovery: a recovery system that causes a rocket to tumble, which increases its drag and slows it down.

That's why sharks and dolphins are streamlined. Their shape reduces drag and makes it easier for them to cut through water quickly.

Several rocket recovery systems use drag to land safely. The simplest system is **tumble recovery**. Generally, a tumble recovery system is used only for very light model rockets. To be able to use this type of recovery system, a rocket's motor must be free to move back in the body tube.

SLOWLY THE ROCKET TUMBLES DOWN!

How does tumble recovery work? After launch, a rocket burns through its propellant as it shoots into the air. A few seconds after the propellant is used, when the rocket reaches its apex, an **ejection charge** fires. The charge causes the rocket's motor to move back in the body tube, or ejects it completely.

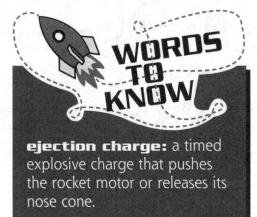

WORDS TO KNOW

ejection charge: a timed explosive charge that pushes the rocket motor or releases its nose cone.

SAFE LANDING!

The change in the motor's position causes the rocket to become unstable. Instead of flying a straight path into the ground, the rocket begins to tumble as it descends.

THE TUMBLING MOVEMENT CAUSES MORE OF THE ROCKET'S SURFACE AREA TO HIT THE FLOWING AIR. THIS CREATES MORE DRAG AND SLOWS THE ROCKET.

COMING BACK TO EARTH:
ROCKET RECOVERY SYSTEMS

Some model rockets use streamers to create drag. When the ejection charge fires, it blows the nose cone off the rocket. The nose cone is still attached to the rocket by a long piece of elastic cord. Streamers are attached to the nose cone. When the cone blows off the rocket body, the streamers unfurl, creating drag to slow the rocket as it descends.

Streamers can be made from paper, plastic, or **Mylar**. Because streamers are not fireproof, the rocket often has fireproof paper called **recovery wadding** stuffed into the body tube. This protects the streamers from the ejection charge's heat.

One of the most popular drag recovery systems uses parachutes, which slow an object as it falls. A parachute fills up with air and pulls in the opposite direction of a falling object's motion. When an ejection charge blows the nose cone off a rocket's body, the nose cone pulls a parachute out of the rocket body. The chute is either attached to the rocket body directly or attached to the nose cone. The chute fills with air and slows the rocket's descent, so that it has a smooth and controlled landing.

DID YOU KNOW?

The space shuttle is the only spacecraft that can carry its payload into space and return it safely back to Earth.

93

Parachutes are most often used for small model rockets, but they can also be used for heavier rockets. The size of the parachute simply increases with the size of the rocket. In fact, all of the manned spacecraft until the space shuttle used parachute recovery systems.

> **TODAY, THE SPACE SHUTTLE'S SOLID ROCKET BOOSTERS USE PARACHUTE RECOVERY SYSTEMS.**

LIFT RECOVERY SYSTEMS

Some recovery systems use lift to land a rocket safely. Lift is an aerodynamic force that opposes the weight of an object moving through the air, holding the object in the air. Lift is produced by the motion of the object through the air. For an airplane, most of the lift is generated by its wings. Recovery systems that increase lift will slow a rocket down so that it can land safely.

DID YOU KNOW?

The five U.S. space shuttles have been named Atlantis, Challenger, Columbia, Discovery, and Endeavour.

A boost **glider** system uses a glider attached to a rocket. First, the rocket launches the glider. At a certain point, an ejection charge separates the glider from the rocket. The glider glides down to Earth while the rocket returns safely using a drag-based recovery system.

The space shuttle uses a boost glider recovery system. When the shuttle returns to Earth's atmosphere, it uses rockets to slow its fall. A special speed brake increases drag and helps to slow down the shuttle as it descends.

WORDS TO KNOW

glider: an aircraft that flies by floating and rising on air currents instead of by engine power.

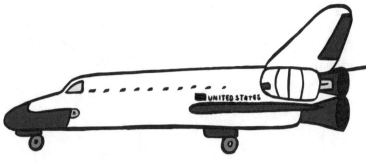

When the shuttle reaches about 185 knots per second (95 miles per second), it releases a drag parachute. The chute increases drag and slows the orbiter. The shuttle's orbiter lands by gliding to the ground. When it lands, the orbiter rolls to a stop.

jettison: to throw something away.

The shuttle's solid rocket boosters use a parachute recovery system. After the boosters are **jettisoned** from the main rocket, parachutes stabilize and slow their descent into the Atlantic Ocean, where the boosters are recovered by special recovery vessels. The boosters can be reused on future shuttle flights.

COLUMBIA TRAGEDY

On February 1, 2003, the space shuttle *Columbia* broke up as it attempted to re-enter Earth's atmosphere. An investigation into the accident discovered that a piece of insulating foam had broken away from the external fuel tank when the shuttle launched from Kennedy Space Center two weeks earlier. The broken piece of foam had hit the edge of the shuttle's left wing and knocked off several heat-resistant tiles that protected the shuttle's wing. When a shuttle re-enters Earth's atmosphere, friction between the atmosphere and the shuttle's surface generates heat. Without the tiles to protect the wing, the superheated air melted part of the wing structure and the wing failed. *Columbia* broke apart, and its entire crew of seven astronauts died.

PROTECT THE PAYLOAD

Rocket designers must create recovery systems that can return scientific instruments and astronauts safely to Earth. In this project, you will design a recovery system that protects your payload—a raw egg—and returns it to Earth unharmed.

1 Design a capsule for your payload using a piece of an egg carton and packing material.

2 Build a parachute from the plastic trash bag and attach it to the capsule using string and tape.

3 **Spread a tarp or other cover on the floor.** You need to protect the surface in case your capsule doesn't work! Mark a landing site on the tarp.

4 Put your payload—a raw egg—into the capsule.

5 Carry it to the top of the ladder or balcony over the landing site.

6 Release the capsule. Using a stopwatch, time how long it takes to reach the landing site. What do you think happened to the egg?

7 Examine the capsule and the egg. If the egg did not crack, you have successfully brought the payload to Earth safely.

Try This: Repeat the project using different capsule designs, packing materials, and parachute designs. Which design produces the safest landing? Which design does not work well?

SUPPLIES

⌒ egg carton
⌒ packing material such as foam, bubble wrap, quilt batting, and newspaper
⌒ scissors
⌒ plastic trash bag
⌒ string
⌒ masking tape
⌒ tarp or other cover for the floor
⌒ raw eggs
⌒ ladder or balcony
⌒ stopwatch

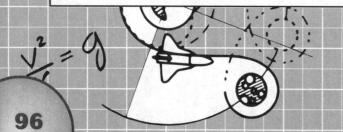

$$\frac{v^2}{r} = g$$

PARACHUTE RECOVERY SYSTEM

Some rockets use parachutes to help the rocket land safely. Parachutes fill with air and create drag, which acts to slow the rocket's movement through the air. In this project, you will see how different parachute designs affect the descent of a foam rocket. Start a scientific method worksheet in your science journal.

1 Drop your rocket from the top of a ladder or balcony to a target below. Have an assistant record the time it takes for the rocket to reach the ground. How did it fall? Record your observations.

2 Cut a parachute from the plastic trash bag. Attach the parachute to the end of the rocket using string and tape. Drop the rocket. Time its descent. Did adding the parachute change how the rocket fell?

3 Repeat the experiment using different parachute designs and sizes. Record your observations each time. How do the different designs affect your results?

Try This: Change the material you use for the parachute. Try paper or fabric. Does using a different material change your results?

DID YOU KNOW?

So far, rockets have come from the space programs in just seven countries—the United States, Russia, Europe, China, Japan, Israel, and India. This may change in the future.

$$v = \sqrt{G\frac{M}{r}}$$

STREAMER RECOVERY SYSTEM

Some model rockets use streamers to help the rocket land safely. Streamers create drag, which acts to slow the rocket's movement through the air. A slower landing generally causes less damage to the rocket. In this project, you will see how adding streamers affects the descent of a foam rocket. Start a scientific method worksheet in your science journal.

SUPPLIES

- science journal and pencil
- foam rocket
- ladder or balcony
- stopwatch
- scissors
- paper
- plastic bags
- duct tape

1 Drop your rocket from the top of a ladder or balcony to a target below. Record the time it takes for the rocket to reach the ground. How did it fall? Record your observations.

2 Cut several paper streamers and attach them to the end of the rocket. Drop the rocket and time its descent. Did adding the streamers change how the rocket fell?

3 Repeat the experiment using streamers made from a plastic bag. Does the different material change your results?

Try This: Vary the number and length of the streamers. Try using different materials. Which streamer design produces the slowest descent?

$$v = \sqrt{G\frac{M}{r}}$$

$$\frac{v^2}{r} = g$$

CHAPTER 7

ROCKETS AT WORK

Rocketry has evolved tremendously since the early Chinese fire arrows. Our understanding of the science of rocketry has allowed engineers to build more reliable rockets that can travel farther and work more effectively than rockets of the past. Today's amazing rockets are used in many ways, from satellites to space flight. In the future, scientists hope that new rocket technologies will be able to propel humans to new horizons in space.

LAUNCHING SATELLITES

Today's rockets carry satellite payloads into orbit around Earth. Satellites are part of your daily life, even if you cannot see them. If you make a long-distance phone call or watch satellite television, you are using a communications satellite that was put into orbit by a rocket.

Before satellites, it was difficult to communicate over a long distance. Signals to radios, televisions, and other communications devices travel in a straight line. A signal from Los Angeles cannot bend and follow the curve of the earth's surface to reach its destination in Athens, Greece.

DID YOU KNOW?

The rocket that has been used the most in the current U.S. space program is the Delta II. It has launched hundreds of satellites into space and is still in use today.

Communications satellites allow radio, television, and telephone signals to travel easily around the world. A signal travels a straight line into space, where it bounces off a satellite, and is redirected to another satellite or back down to its destination on Earth. Communications satellites receive, amplify, and re-broadcast signals to Earth.

You also use satellites when you follow directions using **global positioning system (GPS)**. GPS is a series of about 30 satellites that orbit the earth. Each satellite sends information about its position and the time at regular intervals. These signals travel to a GPS receiver, such as a cell phone, which

WORDS TO KNOW

global positioning system (GPS): a system of satellites, computers, and receivers that determine the location of a receiver on Earth. This is done by calculating the time difference for signals from different satellites to reach the receiver.

calculates how far away you are from each satellite. When the receiver has information from at least three satellites, it can calculate where you are. When might GPS be useful?

Rockets carry other satellites into orbit that are specifically designed to observe the earth. Scientists use observation satellites to monitor the **environment**, forecast weather, and create accurate maps. Weather satellites take pictures of the earth's atmosphere. They monitor clouds, cloud systems, snow cover, storms, ice maps, pollution, and other environmental data. This information is used by forecasters to predict weather. Other satellites track changes in the earth's **vegetation**, atmospheric gas content, ocean color, and ice fields.

WORDS TO KNOW

environment: a natural area with animals, plants, rocks, soil, and water.

vegetation: all the plant life in an area.

POINTED IN THE RIGHT DIRECTION

Not only do rockets put satellites into orbit, rocket power also helps them stay in position. Little rockets called attitude-control thrusters can rotate or tilt a satellite so that its antennae and instruments point in the right direction. Orbit-control thrusters can change the satellite's path or position.

MANNED SPACEFLIGHT

Rockets launch some of the most exciting space missions, such as sending manned spacecraft into outer space. In 1961, Russian cosmonaut Yuri Gagarin was the first human launched into space.

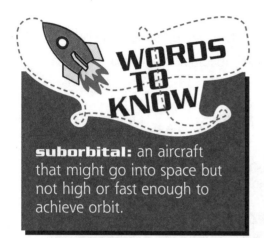

American astronauts quickly followed, with Alan Shepard taking a **suborbital** flight in 1961. In 1962, John Glenn became the first American to orbit the earth. China is the only country besides the United States and Russia to launch a human into space.

In the 1960s, Project Apollo in the United States chased the ultimate goal— placing a man on the moon. To get there, NASA used the Saturn V rocket. The three-stage launch vehicle was powerful enough to send a spacecraft carrying three astronauts into outer space. The project launched several unmanned, robotic flights to test the system and make sure it was safe for humans. Then it launched several test flights, both manned and unmanned, to test how the rocket and the modules it carried worked.

IN 1968, *APOLLO 8* BECAME THE FIRST U.S. MISSION TO ORBIT THE MOON.

DID YOU KNOW?

A launch vehicle is a rocket designed to lift something else into space, such as a satellite or a space probe.

SOUNDING ROCKETS

One of the first modern uses of rockets was to explore the upper atmosphere. This exploration is called sounding. The first U.S. rocket developed for sounding was the WAC-Corporal in 1945. In 1947, a new sounding rocket, the Aerobee, was launched. The Aerobee carried scientific instruments into the upper atmosphere. It also carried some of the first living creatures—monkeys and mice—and took color photographs of Earth. For more than 38 years, the Aerobee helped scientists learn more about the upper atmosphere. Since the Aerobee, many countries have launched sounding rockets for scientific research.

SPACESHIPONE

In 2004, the rocket-powered *SpaceShipOne* was the first privately built spacecraft to carry a human into space. It flew to an altitude of 62 miles (100 kilometers) above the Mojave Desert. *SpaceShipOne* began its trip carried by a specially built airplane. At an altitude of nine miles, the jet engine dropped away. The rocket engine fired and *SpaceShipOne* blasted away.

PS Look at pictures of *SpaceShipOne*. Do you think it's important for civilians to have opportunities to fly into space?

The following year, on July 16, 1969, *Apollo 11* launched from Kennedy Space Center in Florida. *Apollo 11* carried American astronauts Buzz Aldrin and Neil Armstrong, who became the first people to land on the moon. Since the first moon landing, rockets have continued to carry manned spacecraft, including the space shuttle, into outer space.

MILITARY ROCKETS AND MISSILES

From Chinese fire arrows to German V-2 rockets to modern missiles, rockets have been fired as military weapons throughout the years. While a simple rocket travels where it is pointed, a more sophisticated guided missile has a guidance system that directs it to a specific target.

Rockets carry **space probes** and telescopes into outer space to study planets and other objects in space. A space probe is a scientific space exploration mission that is usually unmanned and operated robotically. Several countries, including the United States, Russia, and Japan, have launched space probes to planets and moons in our **solar system**. Space probes have also studied asteroids and comets.

There are several types of military missiles. Surface-to-air missiles fire from the ground to attack and shoot down airplanes. A surface-to-surface missile fires from the ground to another ground target. The German V-2 is an example of a surface-to-surface missile. An air-to-air missile fires from an aircraft against another aircraft, while air-to-ground missiles are fired from aircraft to a ground target.

In 2012, the United States **deployed** the Advanced Precision Kill Weapon System (APKWS) with several Marine Corps units in Afghanistan. The APKWS is a laser-guided rocket that can be fired off an aerial vehicle. It combines a 2.75-inch (7-centimeter) unguided rocket with laser-targeting technology. Military officials believe that this technology makes the rocket more precise in finding its target, which causes fewer **civilian casualties** during an air strike.

WORDS TO KNOW

space probe: a scientific space exploration mission that is usually unmanned and operated robotically.

solar system: the collection of eight planets and their moons in orbit around the sun, together with smaller bodies in the form of asteroids, meteoroids, comets, and dwarf planets.

deploy: to move into position for military action.

civilian: a person who is not in the military.

casualty: someone killed or injured.

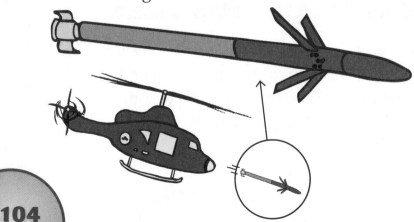

NEW ROCKET FUELS

Rocket scientists are exploring new technologies that will make rockets more efficient, more effective, and more accurate than ever before. Much of this research focuses on new fuels. Generating enough power to lift a rocket and its payload is a tremendous task. Today's chemical rockets use large amounts of propellant to lift heavy payloads into space. Once a spacecraft reaches orbit, most of its propellant is used.

FOR LONGER MISSIONS IN SPACE, NEW FUELS AND PROPULSION SYSTEMS ARE NEEDED.

WORDS TO KNOW

ion: an **atom** with a positive or negative electrical charge. This means it has an extra electron or is missing an electron.

atom: the smallest particle of matter that cannot be broken down by chemical means. An atom is made up of a nucleus of protons and neutrons, surrounded by a cloud of electrons.

ionize: to produce ions.

One promising idea for propelling a rocket is **ion** propulsion. A traditional rocket creates thrust by pushing exhaust gases out of a nozzle at high speed. Ion propulsion is a technology that **ionizes** a gas to propel spacecraft.

The gas xenon is given an electrical charge to ionize it. The ions are then accelerated through a series of negative and positive grids and ejected from the end of the spacecraft, just like exhaust gas. Ion propulsion has several advantages. The mass of the ions is very low compared to the mass of chemical propellants. This means spacecraft using ion propulsion could travel a long distance on a small amount of fuel.

POSITIVE ION **POSITIVE GRID**
ACCELERATED POSITIVE IONS (thrust)
ELECTRON **NEGATIVE GRID**

105

ION PROPULSION WOULD ALLOW A SPACECRAFT TO FUNCTION FOR MONTHS OR YEARS AT A TIME.

The drawback with ion propulsion is that it creates a very low thrust. Ion propulsion would not be able to generate enough thrust to launch a large rocket from Earth into space. This type of system would work best for a rocket already in space.

Other scientists are exploring how to use **nuclear power** to propel rockets for long-term missions. **Fusion** rockets use the energy released when the **nucleus** of one atom is combined with the nucleus of another atom. Fusion releases enormous amounts of energy that could propel a spacecraft.

WORDS TO KNOW

nuclear power: power produced by splitting or fusing atoms.

fusion: a combination or mixture. Nuclear fusion is when the nuclei of two atoms combine.

nucleus: the central part of an atom. Plural is nuclei.

SOLAR SAILS

One day, solar sails may propel rockets in space. A solar sail pushes a spacecraft forward using light from the sun. Light is made of packets of energy called photons. When a beam of light points at a bright, mirror-like surface, the photons reflect back like a ball bouncing off a wall. As they bounce, the photons transmit their momentum to the surface by hitting the surface and reflecting back. This momentum slowly pushes the surface forward.

In 2005, *Cosmos 1* was launched to test solar sail technology. Two private space exploration groups sponsored the spacecraft. The test was never completed, however, because the rocket carrying *Cosmos 1* failed to launch. In the future, scientists hope to build and test a new solar sail spacecraft.

Scientists are also testing lasers to power rockets. Instead of propelling a rocket with chemical reactions onboard, laser propulsion propels a rocket by shining lasers at it from the ground. Lasers heat the air until it explodes and propels the rocket forward. The spacecraft uses mirrors to receive and focus the laser beams. Using lasers as an energy source can reduce the need to carry rocket boosters and onboard propellants, which would make the spacecraft lighter and faster.

ROCKETS OF THE FUTURE

NASA scientists are also working on new rocket designs. They hope these rockets will make it possible to send humans deeper into space than ever before. One rocket in development is NASA's Space Launch System (SLS). It is an advanced heavy-lift launch vehicle that will be the most powerful rocket in history. It will be able to carry the *Orion* Multi-Purpose Crew Vehicle as well as other important cargo, equipment, and science experiments into deep space.

DID YOU KNOW?

The Orion spacecraft can hold up to four astronauts on long-duration, deep space missions, allowing them to explore asteroids, the moon, and eventually Mars.

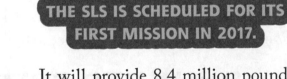

THE SLS IS SCHEDULED FOR ITS FIRST MISSION IN 2017.

It will provide 8.4 million pounds (3.8 million kilograms) of thrust at liftoff and carry 154,000 pounds (70,000 kilograms) of payload. After the first launch, NASA engineers plan to modify the SLS into an even more powerful rocket that will be able to lift 286,000 pounds (130,000 kilograms).

COMMERCIAL SPACE FLIGHT

What's more intense than flying on a jet airplane? How about taking a flight into space? That's exactly what a company called Virgin Galactic plans to do. It's testing a new space plane called *SpaceShipTwo* that will be able to carry tourists into space for suborbital flights. These flights would not fully orbit Earth, but they would give passengers a short experience of weightlessness and a view of Earth from space.

DID YOU KNOW?

To date, more than 650 people have signed up to ride the space flight on SpaceShipTwo. Tickets cost between $200,000 and $250,000 each!

To launch, *SpaceShipTwo* is hooked beneath a carrier airplane. The plane carries *SpaceShipTwo* to an altitude of approximately 50,000 feet (15,240 meters) and releases it in midair. Once released, *SpaceShipTwo* fires its rocket engine, which propels it into space.

UNLIMITED POTENTIAL

The discoveries made by scientists in the past transformed simple rockets into complex vehicles that can launch people and other payloads into outer space. As scientists and engineers continue to study rocketry and develop new tools, fuels, and designs, rockets will blast farther than ever into the universe. How far do you think we can go?

$$\frac{v^2}{r} = g$$

SUPPLIES

- ☊ Internet access
- ☊ paper and pencil
- ☊ craft supplies to build a 3-dimensional model

ROCKET OF THE FUTURE

Through the years, rockets have been used in many ways. In the future, the possibilities are unlimited. Now it's your turn to become a rocket scientist. In this project, you will design your own rocket of the future. You may design a rocket that could be used by the government, scientists, the military, or individuals. What will you create for the future?

1 Brainstorm several ideas for new uses for rockets. For inspiration, you may want to research rockets on the Internet. After you have a good list of ideas, choose one that you want to develop further.

2 Once you have decided the kind of rocket you want to develop, consider what the rocket will look like. What components will it have? How will it be powered? What need does it fill? Will it be used by government, schools, or individuals? How will it be used?

3 Create an illustration or **prototype** of your rocket. Present information about its systems and special characteristics. Now build a 3-D model of your rocket. Use trial and error to build and test it.

Try This: What problems do you anticipate may occur with your new rocket? What can you do during design to reduce these problems?

WORDS TO KNOW

prototype: a working model or mock-up that allows engineers to test their solution.

$$v = \sqrt{G\frac{M}{r}}$$

GLOSSARY

accelerate: to change the speed of an object over time.

active control system: controls that can be moved during flight to stabilize and steer a rocket.

adjacent: next to.

aeolipile: a spinning ball invented by Greek mathematician Hero that uses steam to move.

aerodynamics: the movement of air and other gases around an object.

aeronautics: the science of flight.

air resistance: the frictional force that acts on an object as it travels through the air.

alchemy: an early form of chemistry with the goal of turning ordinary metals into gold.

altitude: the height of something in relation to sea level.

apex: the highest point of something.

arc: a curved path.

artificial satellite: a manmade object that orbits around the earth or the moon.

artillery: large guns used to shoot over a great distance.

asphyxiate: to die from lack of oxygen.

astronaut: a person trained for spaceflight.

astronomical: having to do with things in outer space.

astronomy: the study of the stars, planets, and space.

atmosphere: the blanket of air surrounding the earth.

atom: the smallest particle of matter that cannot be broken down by chemical means. An atom is made up of a nucleus of protons and neutrons, surrounded by a cloud of electrons.

ballistics: the science that studies the movement of objects that are shot through the air.

ballistic missile: a missile that is at first powered and guided but is then pulled by gravity to its target.

ballistic trajectory: the trajectory of an object acted upon by only gravity and drag.

bamboo: a tree-like type of grass with a hollow, woody stem.

BCE: put after a date, BCE stands for Before Common Era and counts down to zero. CE stands for Common Era and counts up from zero. These non-religious terms correspond to BC and AD.

booster: a rocket used to give another craft the power needed for takeoff.

burn rate: a measure of how fast a solid propellant burns.

canards: small movable fins attached near the nose of a rocket that can be tilted during flight.

GLOSSARY

cargo: goods or materials that are carried or transported by a vehicle.

casualty: someone killed or injured.

center of mass (CM): the point on an object where its mass is equally balanced on both sides.

center of pressure (CP): the point on an object in the air where the drag and lift forces acting on it are equal.

chemical reaction: the change of a substance into a new substance.

civilian: a person who is not in the military.

combustion: the process of burning.

combustion chamber: the part of a rocket where liquid fuel and oxidizer are combined to create a chemical reaction.

combustion products: hot, expanding gases produced from a chemical reaction between a fuel and an oxidizer in a rocket engine.

commercially: made by a business.

component: an important part of a system or mixture.

compress: to squeeze and squish something to make it smaller.

condense: to change from a gas to a liquid, which makes the substance more dense or compact.

cosmonaut: a Russian astronaut.

deploy: to move into position for military action.

drag: the resistance air exerts on a body moving through it.

ejection charge: a timed explosive charge that pushes the rocket motor or releases its nose cone.

energy: the ability to do work.

engineering: using science and math to design and build things.

environment: a natural area with animals, plants, rocks, soil, and water.

erratic: moving in an irregular pattern.

euthanize: to put to death without pain.

exert: to make an intense action or effort.

exhaust gases: the hot gases produced from a rocket's engine.

exhaust velocity: the speed at which gas escapes from a rocket.

expel: to drive or push out.

force: a push or pull that changes the speed or direction of an object.

foundation: the basis of something.

friction: a force that slows down objects when they rub against each other.

fuel: a material used to produce heat or power.

GLOSSARY

fuse: a cord used to set an explosive on fire.

fuselage: the central part of a rocket or spacecraft where the crew, cargo, or other payload is located.

fusion: a combination or mixture. Nuclear fusion is when the nuclei of two atoms combine.

gimbaled nozzle: a nozzle that can swivel from side to side, changing the direction of the engine's thrust to adjust its flight path.

glider: an aircraft that flies by floating and rising on air currents instead of by engine power.

global positioning system (GPS): a system of satellites, computers, and receivers that determine the location of a receiver on Earth. This is done by calculating the time difference for signals from different satellites to reach the receiver.

gravity: the force that holds objects on the ground.

guidance system: all of the parts that help a rocket control its flight, including computers, sensors, and radar.

guided missile: a self-propelled missile that can be steered in flight by remote control or by an onboard homing device.

gyroscope: a spinning wheel that is used to help control a rocket in flight.

hollow core: an empty space inside a tube.

igniter: something that sets a substance on fire.

inertia: the tendency of matter to either stay at rest or stay in motion unless acted upon by a force.

infrastructure: basic facilities such as roads, power plants, and communication systems.

insulated: covered with a material that limits the transfer of heat.

ion: an atom with a positive or negative electrical charge. This means it has an extra electron or is missing an electron.

ionize: to produce ions.

jettison: to throw something away.

launch: to fire up into the air.

launch pad: the platform from which a rocket launches.

lift: an aerodynamic force that pushes upward on an object in flight.

manned spacecraft: a spacecraft that carries humans.

mass: the amount of matter in an object.

GLOSSARY

mass fraction (MF): a calculation used to measure the balance between payload and range, which is the effectiveness of a rocket's design.

matter: anything that has weight and takes up space.

metric: relating to or using the metric system of measurement, which is based on units of 10.

missile: an object or weapon that is propelled toward a target.

Mongols: a group of wandering tribes led by Genghis Khan that lived to the north of China.

motion: the act or process of moving.

movable fins: fins attached to a rocket that can be tilted to stabilize a rocket.

multi-stage rocket: a rocket that is made up of smaller rockets that detach as their fuel is used up.

Mylar: a strong, very thin film of polyester.

net force: a force that is the result of two or more forces acting together.

nomadic: moving from place to place each season in search of food and water.

nozzle: a narrow opening at the base of a rocket that controls the flow of exhaust gases from its engine.

nuclear power: power produced by splitting or fusing atoms.

nucleus: the central part of an atom. Plural is nuclei.

opposing force: a force that acts in a pair against another force.

optics: the science of visible and invisible light.

orbit: the path of an object circling another object in space.

orbiter: a spacecraft designed to orbit a planet or moon without landing on its surface.

oxidizer: a substance that contains oxygen that mixes with fuel in a rocket engine to help it burn.

parallel staging: a setup in which several small rockets are strapped to the sides of a central rocket and fired at launch, then discarded after their propellant is used.

passive control system: fixed controls that stabilize a rocket.

payload: the cargo of a rocket, such as an explosive charge, instruments, or astronauts.

payload system: something a rocket carries, such as a satellite, astronaut, equipment, or weapons.

physics: the science of matter, motion, force, and energy.

plague: an infectious disease that causes many deaths.

pressure: the force that pushes on an object.

GLOSSARY

principle: the basic way that something works.

propel: to drive or move forward.

propellant: a combination of fuel and oxidizer that burns to produce thrust in a rocket.

propulsion system: the parts needed to propel a rocket.

prototype: a working model or mock-up that allows engineers to test their solution.

radar: a device that detects objects by bouncing radio waves off them and measuring how long it takes for the waves to return.

range: the distance a rocket can travel.

recovery system: the parts of a rocket that help it return safely to Earth.

recovery wadding: fireproof material that is stuffed into the body of a rocket to protect recovery systems and payload from heat.

resistance: a force that slows down another force.

robot probe: a machine that travels into space to find out more about space and send information back to the earth.

rocket: a machine that pushes itself forward by pushing out material such as hot gas.

rocketeer: a person who designs, launches, operates, or travels in a space rocket.

rocketry: the design, construction, operation, and launching of rockets.

rotate: to turn like a wheel around a fixed point.

saltpeter: a white powder found in Chinese caves that was used in early Chinese gunpowder.

satellite: an object that orbits another object in space.

serial staging: a setup in which several small rockets are stacked on top of each other in stages. Each is fired in order and discarded when its propellant is used.

solar system: the collection of eight planets and their moons in orbit around the sun, together with smaller bodies in the form of asteroids, meteoroids, comets, and dwarf planets.

space probe: a scientific space exploration mission that is usually unmanned and operated robotically.

speed of sound: the speed at which sound travels. In the air at sea level, this is 755 miles per hour (1,215 kilometers per hour).

sphere: round, like a ball.

stabilize: to make reliable and steady.

stable: reliable and steady.

GLOSSARY

stage: a smaller rocket that is stacked with other rockets and detaches when its fuel is used up.

streamline: with smooth lines to reduce resistance.

structural system: a rocket's frame, body, and fins.

suborbital: an aircraft that might go into space but not high or fast enough to achieve orbit.

surface area: the parts of an object that are on the surface.

tangent of the angle: the length of the opposite side of the triangle divided by the length of the adjacent side of the triangle.

technology: tools, methods, and systems used to solve a problem or do work.

terminology: the important words used in a specific subject.

theology: the study of religion or ideas about religion.

thermal: having to do with heat.

thrust: the force created when gas escapes from a rocket's engine.

trial and error: trying first one thing, then another and another, until something works.

tribe: a large group of people with common ancestors and customs.

tumble: to fall helplessly, turning over and over.

tumble recovery: a recovery system that causes a rocket to tumble, which increases its drag and slows it down.

unbalanced force: a force that has no partner force of equal power acting on it in the opposite direction.

universe: everything that exists everywhere.

unstable: not steady, unpredictable.

vacuum: a space in which there is no air.

vanes: small fins placed inside a rocket's exhaust pipe that add stability.

vegetation: all the plant life in an area.

vehicle: a machine that moves people and things from one place to another.

velocity: the rate at which an object is moving.

vernier rocket: a very small rocket used to make exact adjustments to the flight of a large rocket.

volume: the amount of space an object takes up.

warhead: the part of a missile that holds an explosive charge.

weight: the product of the mass of an object and the force of gravity acting on the object.

working fluid: a liquid or gas substance that operates an engine.

RESOURCES

BOOKS

Rockets. Joseph A. Angelo Jr., Facts On File, 2006.

How Does a Rocket Work? Sarah Eason, Gareth Stevens Publishing, 2010.

Rockets. Ron Miller, Lerner Books, 2008.

Rockets. Steven Otfinoski, Marshall Cavendish Publishing, 2007.

Space Exploration for Dummies. Cynthia Phillips and
Shana Priwer, Wiley Publishing, 2009.

*It's ONLY Rocket Science: An Introduction in Plain
English.* Lucy Rogers, Springer, 2008.

*This is Rocket Science: True Stories of the Risk-Taking Scientists Who Figure Out
Ways to Explore Beyond Earth.* Gloria Skurzynski, National Geographic, 2010.

MUSEUMS AND SCIENCE CENTERS

Kennedy Space Center, Orlando, Florida
kennedyspacecenter.com
At the center, visitors can touch moon rocks, meet veteran NASA astronauts,
explore spacecraft, and experience numerous interactive exhibits.

Smithsonian National Air and Space Museum, Washington, DC
airandspace.si.edu
The museum has exhibits and artifacts relating to
the history of flight and space flight.

Space Center Houston, Houston, Texas
spacecenter.org
The gateway to the Johnson Space Center, it has many exhibits,
artifacts, and films related to the United States' space program.

U.S. Space & Rocket Center, Huntsville, Alabama
rocketcenter.com
The U.S. Space & Rocket Center is recognized as one of the most
comprehensive U.S. manned space flight hardware museums in the world.

RESOURCES

WEBSITES

National Aeronautics and Space Administration (NASA)
nasa.gov
Information about the history of the U.S. space program,
the science of rocketry, and current NASA programs.

National Association of Rocketry
nar.org/about.html
The website for the oldest and largest sport rocketry organization
in the world, dedicated to safety, youth education, and the
advancement of model rocketry. The group hosts amateur
launches and competitions throughout the year.

Physics 4 Kids
physics4kids.com/files/motion_laws.html
Explains Newton's laws of motion and other
scientific concepts for students.

Victorian Space Science Education Centre
vssec.vic.edu.au
This website has many articles about rocketry and sample
activities for students.

PRIMARY SOURCE QR CODES

page 4: *sciencekids.co.nz/videos/space/shuttlelaunch.html*

page 19: *youtube.com/watch?v=RMINSD7MmT4&feature=kp*

page 29: *cudl.lib.cam.ac.uk/view/MS-ADD-03958/158*

page 38: *hubblesite.org*

page 79: *youtube.com/watch?v=csMTPjl-rhc*

page 103: *virgingalactic.com/multimedia/album/whiteknightone-and-spaceshipone*

INDEX

INDEX

INDEX